The Heart of Christianity

Ron Rhodes

HARVEST HOUSE PUBLISHERS
Eugene, Oregon 97402

THE HEART OF CHRISTIANITY
Copyright © 1996 by Harvest House Publishers
Eugene, Oregon 97402

Rhodes, Ron.
      The heart of Christianity / Ron Rhodes.
            p. cm.
      Includes bibliographical references.
      ISBN 1-56507-463-7 (alk. paper)
      1. Christianity—Essence, genius, nature. 2. Jesus Christ—Knowableness. 3. Jesus
Christ—Person and offices. 4. Christian life. I. Title.
BT60.R56 1996
230—dc20   96-11197
                                                                                                          CIP

Printed in the United States of America.

96 97 98 99 00 01 02 / BF / 10 9 8 7 6 5 4 3 2 1

To Earl and JoAnne Stout—
with appreciation
for your love and support over the years

Acknowledgments

As was true with my previous books, my wife Kerri deserves special mention. Besides being a great encourager as well as proofreader, she's been an enormous help in the organization I recently founded, Reasoning from the Scriptures Ministries. I consider myself incredibly blessed to be married to her!

My two children, David and Kylie, have also been a wonderful encouragement during the writing of this book. I'm especially appreciative of the rest breaks they provided. David, it was fun watching all your soccer games. Kylie, I enjoyed seeing you in action in your gymnastics class.

Finally, I'm thankful to the entire staff of Harvest House Publishers. They're a pleasure to work with. Here I want to single out Mary Cooper, who first approached me regarding the need for a book on "the heart of Christianity." Thanks, Mary!

Contents

"Christianity is not devotion to work, or to a cause,
or a doctrine, but devotion to a person,
the Lord Jesus Christ."
— *Oswald Chambers*

"Christianity isn't only going to church
on Sunday. It is living twenty-four hours of
every day with Jesus Christ."
— *Billy Graham*

"Christianity is not the acceptance
of certain ideas. It is a personal attitude of trust and
devotion to a person."
— *Stephen Neill*

"A Christian is, in essence,
somebody personally related to Jesus Christ.
Christianity without Christ is a chest
without a treasure, a frame without a portrait."
— *John R.W. Stott*

**In short,
Jesus is the heart of
Christianity.**

A Relationship with Jesus —
The Heart of Christianity

A relationship with Jesus is the heart of Christianity. Without Jesus there would be no Christianity.

From a biblical perspective, to *know* Jesus is to know God. To *see* Jesus is to see God. To *believe* in Jesus is to believe in God. To *receive* Jesus is to receive God. To *honor* Jesus is to honor God. To *worship* Jesus is to worship God. A relationship with Jesus, then, is the most important relationship you can have.

Since a relationship with Jesus is the very heart of Christianity, it follows that the major doctrines (or teachings) of Christianity—including the doctrines of God, man, salvation, the church, angels, and the afterlife—are tied directly to Christ. Christ is the thread that runs through all these doctrines. He ties the whole Bible together. Let's take a look now at how that is.

Jesus Is God

We'll talk a lot about God in this book. And a book about Christianity *should* talk a lot about God.

One thing we'll see is that Jesus Himself *is* God. In fact, He is referred to in the Bible as both "God" (Hebrews 1:8) and "Lord" (Matthew 22:43-45). Jesus has all the attributes (or characteristics) of God. For example, He's *all-powerful* (Matthew 28:18) and *all-knowing* (John 2:24-25). Jesus does things that only God can do—such as creating the entire universe (John 1:3) and raising people from the dead (John 11:43-44). Moreover, Jesus was worshiped as God by the people who came to know Him (Matthew 14:33).

We'll talk a lot more about Jesus in this book. At this point, it's enough to recognize that *Jesus is at the very heart of the doctrine of God.*

Jesus Is the Creator of the Universe

The Old Testament presents God Almighty as the Creator of the universe (Isaiah 44:24). But in the New Testament, Jesus is portrayed as the agent of creation (Colossians 1:16). This confirms for us that Jesus Himself is God.

When we look at the universe around us, then, we see the handiwork of Jesus Christ. He's the one who made it. We catch a glimpse of His majesty and glory as we look at the starry sky above.

Jesus is at the very heart of the doctrine of creation.

Jesus Created Humankind

Jesus didn't just create the universe, He also created humankind (John 1:3). In the Genesis account we read that when the Lord created Adam, He declared Adam's loneliness to be "not good" (Genesis 2:18). The Lord created man to have relationships. He created man as a social being. And since man is a social being, it is not good for him to be alone.

You and I as human beings were created with a need not just for fellowship with other humans (as Adam had a need for Eve) but also with a need for fellowship with God. And we are restless and insecure until a relationship with God becomes our living experience. Christ came into the world *as a man* to make that experience a reality for all who believe in Him.

Jesus is at the very heart of the doctrine of man.

Jesus Is the Ultimate Revelation of God

There are many ways that God has revealed Himself to humankind. For example, God reveals His majesty and glory in the universe around us (Psalm 19). And since Christ Himself created the universe, the revelation in the universe is His doing.

God has also revealed Himself through the mouths of the prophets. First Peter 1:11 tells us that it was the Spirit of Christ who spoke through all the prophets in biblical times. So the revelation that came through them is Christ's doing.

The Bible reveals that the ultimate revelation of God was Jesus Himself. Jesus—as eternal God—took on human flesh so He could be God's fullest revelation to humankind (Hebrews 1:2-3). Jesus was a revelation of God not just in His person (as God) but in His life and teachings as well. By observing the things Jesus did and said, we learn a great deal about God.

Here are just a few of the ways that Jesus revealed God:

• God's awesome power was revealed in Jesus (John 3:2).

• God's incredible wisdom was revealed in Jesus (1 Corinthians 1:24).

• God's boundless love was revealed and demonstrated by Jesus (1 John 3:16).

• God's unfathomable grace was revealed in Jesus (2 Thessalonians 1:12).

All this serves as the backdrop as to why Jesus told a group of Pharisees, "When a man believes in me, he does not believe in me only, but in the one who sent me. When he looks at me, he sees the one who sent me" (John 12:44-45).

Jesus is at the very heart of the doctrine of revelation.

The Bible Is a Jesus Book

From beginning to end, from Genesis to Revelation, the Bible is a Jesus book.

Jesus once told some Jews, "You diligently study the Scriptures because you think that by them you possess eternal life. These are the Scriptures that testify about me, yet you refuse to come to me to have life" (John 5:39-40). The Jews to whom Jesus spoke knew the shell of the Bible but were neglecting the kernel within it. It is not the Book that saves, but the Savior of the Book.

We must ever keep in mind that Jesus said the Scriptures were "concerning himself" (Luke 24:27), were "written about me" (verse 44), were "written of me" (Hebrews 10:7 NASB), and "bear witness to me" (John 5:39 NASB).

Jesus is at the very heart of the doctrine of the Bible.

Jesus Is the Savior

Man's sin against God posed a problem for God. How could He remain holy and just and at the same time forgive the sinner and allow the sinner into His presence? God's ineffable purity cannot tolerate sin. He is of purer eyes than to behold evil. How, then, can the righteous God deal in a just way with the sinner and at the same time satisfy His own compassion and love in saving him from doom?

The answer is found in Jesus. Jesus came as our beloved Savior and died on the cross on our behalf (Matthew 20:28). Jesus our Savior "gave himself as a ransom for all men" (1 Timothy 2:6). Those who believe in Him are forgiven of their sins and their relationship with God is instantly restored (Acts 16:31).

Jesus is at the very heart of the doctrine of salvation.

The Holy Spirit Glorifies Jesus

Just before His crucifixion, Jesus met with the disciples in the Upper Room and gave them some final words of encouragement. During this time, He spoke to them about the coming of the Holy Spirit.

A primary ministry of the Holy Spirit is to glorify Christ and to make known the things of Christ (John 14:26). The Spirit testifies about Christ (John 15:26). The Spirit does not seek to make Himself prominent, but rather seeks to exalt Jesus Christ.

Jesus is at the very heart of the doctrine of the Holy Spirit.

Jesus Is the Head of the Church

The church is a company of people who have one Lord and who share together in one gift of salvation in the Lord Jesus Christ.

In Matthew 16:18 Jesus affirmed to Peter, "I will build *my* church." The church is not the result of some pastor or priest or body of elders. It is not owned by some denomination. It is Christ Himself who builds the church. The church is His and *His alone*.

Christ not only owns the church, He is also the head of it (Ephesians 5:23). Moreover, Scripture says that Christ "purchased" the church with His own blood upon the cross (Acts 20:28).

Jesus is at the very heart of the doctrine of the church.

The Angels Worship and Serve Jesus

Jesus created the angels (Colossians 1:16). Angels are seen worshiping Jesus in Old Testament times (*see* both Isaiah 6:1-5 and John 12:41). An angel announced the birth of Jesus to Mary (Luke 1:26-28) and to Joseph (Matthew 1:20). Angels proclaimed the birth of Jesus to the shepherds in the field (Luke 2:9). Angels ministered to Jesus during His infancy (Matthew 2:13-18).

Angels also ministered to Jesus during His ministry (Matthew 4:1-11) and just before the crucifixion (Luke 22:43). An angel rolled away the stone following Jesus' resurrection from the dead (Matthew 28:1-6).

Angels appeared when Jesus ascended back into heaven (Acts 1:9-11). When Jesus comes again, He will be accompanied by angels (Matthew 16:27). And finally, the angels will worship and exalt Jesus for all eternity (Revelation 5:11-14).

Jesus is at the very heart of the doctrine of angels.

Jesus Made Eternal Life Possible for Us

Jesus made it possible for you and I to go to heaven. Those who believe in Jesus receive eternal life and will live forever with Him.

Can there be anything more sublime and more utterly satisfying for the Christian than to enjoy the sheer delight of unbroken fellowship with Christ in heaven, and have immediate and completely unobstructed access to Him (2 Corinthians 5:6-8)? We will see our beloved Lord face to face in all His splendor and glory. We will gaze upon His countenance and behold His resplendent beauty forever.

Jesus is truly the heart of the doctrine of the afterlife.

The Heart of the Matter

Do you now see what I mean when I say Jesus is a thread that runs through the entire Bible? Do you now see what I mean when I say that a relationship with Jesus is the heart of Christianity? Truly, Christianity without Christ is like a chest without a treasure.

My friend, my deepest desire and prayer for you is that when you finish this book, you will not only have a better understanding of the major doctrines of Christianity, but also that your personal relationship with Jesus would soar to ever new heights of intimacy. *That, after all, is what true Christianity is all about.*

The Heart of Christianity

A relationship with Jesus is the very heart of Christianity.

Jesus is also the heart of every major doctrine (or teaching) of Christianity, as the chart below illustrates. Truly, Christianity without Christ is like a chest without a treasure, a frame without a portrait.

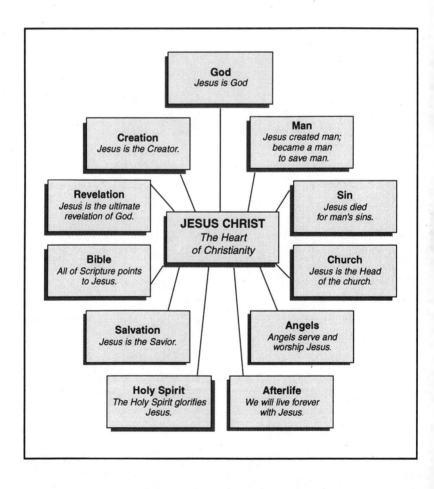

A Christian is a person who has trusted in Christ for salvation and who has a personal relationship with Him.

ONE

Just What Is a Christian Anyway?

In my childhood...and through my teenage years, I thought I was a Christian because I attended church regularly. For years I participated in various church activities, sang in the church choir, and went through all the right motions. I even went through a "confirmation" ceremony at my church—an event that was supposed to confirm my status as a Christian. I had no idea at that time that I really wasn't a Christian according to the biblical definition of the term.

Like so many other people today, I was under the illusion that a Christian is merely a church-attender, or perhaps a person who is fairly consistent in governing his or her life in accordance with a Christian code of ethics. In this line of thinking, a person can look forward to a destiny in heaven as long as his or her good deeds outweigh the bad deeds by the time he or she dies.

It wasn't until years later that I came to understand that the mere act of attending church does not make a person a Christian. As the late great evangelist Billy Sunday (1862-1935) put it, "Going to church doesn't make you a Christian any more than going to a garage makes you an automobile."[1]

At the most basic level, a Christian is a person who has a personal relationship with Jesus Christ. It is a relationship that begins the moment you place faith in Christ for salvation (Acts 16:31). When you believe in Jesus (John 3:16), you start an eternal relationship with Him. (It's eternal because it lasts the rest of your life on earth and then continues forever in heaven after you die.) It is a blessed relationship in which the Christian has the profound privilege of spiritually walking with Jesus on a daily basis, trusting Him to meet each and every need. From a biblical perspective, then, Christianity is not so much a religion as it is a relationship.

We must keep in mind that being a Christian is more than just knowing about Jesus Christ. Becoming a Christian involves *faith* in Christ, and this faith leads to genuine *fellowship* with Christ. "Our fellowship," explained the apostle John, "is with the Father and with his Son, Jesus Christ" (1 John 1:3).

It is fascinating to me that the word *Christian* is used only three times in the New Testament—the most important being Acts 11:26. (The other two verses are Acts 26:28 and 1 Peter 4:16.) It is instructive to observe just what this word meant among those to whom the term was originally applied.

In Acts 11:26, we are told simply and straightforwardly, "The disciples were called Christians first at Antioch." This would have been around A.D. 42, about a decade after Christ died on the cross and rose again from the dead.

Up until this time the followers of Jesus had been known among themselves by such terms as "believers"

(Acts 2:44), "brothers" (Acts 15:1,23), and "disciples" (Acts 9:26). But now, in Antioch, they are called Christians.

What does the term mean? The answer is found in the *-ian* ending. Among the ancients, the *-ian* ending meant "belonging to the party of." *Herodians*, then, belonged to the party of Herod. *Caesarians* belonged to the party of Caesar. Christians belonged to Christ. And Christians were loyal to Christ, just as the Herodians were loyal to Herod and Caesarians were loyal to Caesar.

The significance of the name *Christian* was that these followers of Jesus were recognized as a distinct group. They were seen as distinct from Judaism and from all other religions of the ancient world. We might loosely translate the term *Christian* to mean "one who belongs to Christ," "a Christ-one," or perhaps "Christ-follower." *Christians are people who believe in Christ and have a personal relationship with Him.*

You might find it helpful to ponder what one resident of Antioch might have said to another regarding these committed followers of Jesus: "Who are these people?" The other person would answer, "Oh, these are the people who are always talking about Christ—they are the Christ-people, or the Christians."

Those who have studied the culture of Antioch have noted that the Antiochans were well known for making fun of people. It may be that the early followers of Jesus were initially called Christians by local residents as a term of derision or ridicule. History reveals that by the second century, Christians adopted the title as a badge of honor. They took pride (in a healthy kind of way) in following Jesus. They had a genuine relationship with the living, resurrected Christ and they were utterly faithful to Him, even in the face of death.

That the followers of Jesus were first called Christians in Antioch is highly significant. This city was made up of a

mixture of Jews and Gentiles, and people of both back-
grounds were followers of Jesus. What brought these believers unity was not their race, or culture, or language. Rather,
their unity came from all of them having a relationship
with Jesus. *Christianity crosses all cultural and ethnic bound-
aries.*

What Is Christianity?

If a *Christian* is a person who has a personal relationship
with Jesus, then *Christianity*—at its most basic level—is a
collective group of people who have a personal relationship
with Jesus. As J.I. Packer put it so well, "The essence of
Christianity is neither beliefs nor behavior patterns. It is
the reality of communion here and now with Christianity's
living founder, the Mediator, Jesus Christ."[2] Indeed,
"Christianity is a kind of love affair with our loving Lord
and Savior, and the more days we turn into spiritual
Valentine's Days by talking to the Lord about our relationship with Him…the richer and more joyful the relationship
itself will become."[3]

We should note that there is no instance recorded in
the New Testament of the early Christians referring to their
collective movement as "Christianity," even though the
term *Christian* was used with greater frequency as the movement grew in numbers. By the time of Augustine (A.D.
396-430), the use of the term *Christianity* appears to have
become widespread. It progressively became a term describ-
ing a movement of people who had a personal relationship
with—*and commitment to*—Jesus Christ.

Great Christians down through the centuries have recognized that Christianity most fundamentally involves a
personal relationship with Jesus.

- Devotional writer Oswald Chambers (1874-1917)
  said, "Christianity is not devotion to work, or to a
  cause, or a doctrine, but devotion to a person, the
  Lord Jesus Christ."[4]

- Evangelist Billy Graham (born 1918) said, "Christianity isn't only going to church on Sunday. It is living twenty-four hours of every day with Jesus Christ."[5]

- Bible scholar Stephen Neill said, "Christianity is not the acceptance of certain ideas. It is a personal attitude of trust and devotion to a person."[6]

- Theologian John R.W. Stott said, "A Christian is, in essence, somebody personally related to Jesus Christ."[7]

Why do I focus so much attention on the relational aspect of Christianity? Simply because a personal relationship with Jesus is the heart and soul of Christianity. *Christianity is essentially Christ.* The person and work of Jesus Christ are the rock upon which Christianity is built. If He is not who He said He was, and if He did not do what He said He came to do, the foundation of Christianity is undermined and the whole superstructure collapses.

Take Christ from Christianity, and you disembowel it. There is nothing left. Christ is the heart and center of Christianity. All else is mere circumference. Christianity is not primarily concerned with following Jesus' philosophy of life or seeking to imitate His ethic. Christianity is first and foremost concerned with personally relating to Him.

As I noted in the Introduction, to know Jesus is to know God (John 8:19). To see Jesus is to see God (John 12:45). To believe in Jesus is to believe in God (John 12:44). To receive Jesus is to receive God (Mark 9:37). To honor Jesus is to honor God (John 5:23). To worship Jesus is to worship God (Revelation 4–5). A relationship with Jesus, then, is the most important relationship you can have.

In view of the above, Christianity as a relationship with Christ will be a thread that will run throughout this entire book. Because a personal relationship with Jesus is the heart of true Christianity, Jesus is also at the heart of all the major doctrines (or teachings) of Christianity. I trust that as you read the following pages, you will see—as I came to see years ago—that the Bible is predominantly a Jesus book.

⟶⟋⟍⟵ *A Verse to Hide in Your Heart* ⟶⟋⟍⟵

"Our fellowship is with the Father and with his Son, Jesus Christ."

1 JOHN 1:3

> Knowing God should be our chief aim in life. Jesus has made it possible for us to enter into a living and vibrant relationship with God.

TWO

Knowing God: The Highest Priority

In view of the sheer vastness of the stellar universe, it is truly amazing that God has sovereignly chosen our tiny planet earth as a center of divine activity. Relatively speaking, the earth is but an atom among the whirling constellations, only a tiny speck of dust in the ocean of stars and planets in the universe.

To the naturalistic astronomer, earth is merely one of many planets in our small solar system, all of which are in orbit around the sun. But the earth is not just another planet, it is the center of God's work of salvation in the universe. Indeed, it is on the earth that the eternal Son of God became a man and died on the cross to provide salvation for fallen humanity.[1]

The centrality of the earth is also evident in the creation account, for God created the earth *before* He created the rest of the planets and stars. The earth was created on the first day

(Genesis 1:1); the sun, moon, and stars were created on the fourth (Genesis 1:14-15).

Coming to Know God

God not only made this world, He also created man upon it. And as inscrutable as it may seem to the human mind, God specially constructed man with a capacity to know and fellowship with Him. Our purpose—indeed, our highest aim in life—should be to know God.

"What were we made for? To know God!" said J.I. Packer in his modern classic *Knowing God.* "What aim should we set ourselves in life? To know God. What is the 'eternal life' that Jesus gives? Knowledge of God. 'This is life eternal, that they might know thee, the only true God, and Jesus Christ, whom thou hast sent' (John 17:3). What is the best thing in life, bringing more joy, delight, and contentment, than anything else? Knowledge of God."[2]

We read in Scripture, "This is what the LORD says: 'Let not the wise man boast of his wisdom or the strong man boast of his strength or the rich man boast of his riches, but let him who boasts boast about this: that he understands and knows me'" (Jeremiah 9:23-24).

Knowing Jesus Christ—who Himself is God, and is the full revelation of God to man—takes on similar importance in the New Testament. The apostle Paul said, "I consider everything a loss compared to the surpassing greatness of knowing Christ Jesus my Lord, for whose sake I have lost all things" (Philippians 3:8).

Man Created as a Social Being

When God created Adam, He declared Adam's loneliness to be "not good" (Genesis 2:18). God made man as a social being. Man was not created to be alone. He was created to enter into and enjoy relationships with other people.

The most important relationship man was created to enter into is that with God Himself. There is a hunger in the heart of man that none but God can satisfy, a vacuum that only God can fill. We were created with a need for fellowship with God. And we are restless and insecure until this becomes our living experience.

All this is because God created man in His image (Genesis 1:26). While many people have debated down through the centuries what it means for man to be created in God's image, one thing is certain: Part of that "image" is that man is a personal, social, and relational being. We were made with a capacity to interact with the Creator on a personal level.

Just as God has a social nature, so also has He endowed man with a social nature. And because man has a social nature, man in his deepest heart seeks companionship with his Creator. He yearns for this relationship so that the void in his heart can be filled.

Certainly many people have tried (and will continue to try) to fill that void with earthly things—human relationships, power, prestige, and the like. But until a person comes into the relationship with God that he was created for, the void will remain ever-present.

It seems clear from the Bible that the first man and woman entered into intimate fellowship with God in a very direct way. We read that on one particular day Adam and Eve "heard the sound of the LORD God as he was walking in the garden in the cool of the day" (Genesis 3:8).

I believe this statement implies that God entered the garden on a regular basis. It seems natural to assume that God came into the garden frequently for the sole purpose of fellowshiping with the first man and woman. How blessed it must have been!

God desires to fellowship with you and me, too. As we will see throughout the rest of this book, Jesus Christ has made it possible for us to enter into a living and vibrant spiritual relationship with God (John 14:6).

Knowledge Versus Knowing

I must make an extremely important qualification here. In this chapter I'm not talking about mere intellectual knowledge *about* God or Jesus Christ. I'm talking about personally knowing God and Christ on an intimate level. That is what Christianity is all about.

Knowing Christ is a whole lot more than just knowing some things about Him. A person could have all the right facts in his head without ever tasting in his heart the reality to which he refers.

Knowing God and Christ in the biblical sense is a matter of personal involvement. It involves personal commitment to God's desires, His interests, His concerns, and to fellowshiping with Him. In short, our aim should be not just to understand the *attributes* of God intellectually but to enlarge our personal *acquaintance* with Him.[3]

Knowing what the Bible says about God and Christ is important, but only as long as it helps us to get to know God and Christ better and more intimately. We go to the pages of Scripture not to cram our heads with a bunch of facts but to get to know God on a personal level—and more particularly, Jesus Christ—and learn how to live in a way pleasing to Him.

Obedience to God's Word must not be seen as an end in itself. We must seek to learn God's Word and obey it because we treasure our personal relationship and daily walk with Jesus and do not want it to be hindered by foolish actions on our part. As the psalmist said, "I have hidden your word in my heart *that I might not sin against you*" (Psalm 119:11, emphasis added).

Getting to Know God

Our relationship with God begins the very moment we trust in Christ for salvation. But, of course, *coming to know* God is not possible with just a single encounter. Knowing

God involves a relationship not just of commitment but of time. It is only after loving involvement spent with another that a person comes to actually know another.

That principle is true in human relationships. The only way to get to know a person is to spend time with him or her. And as we spend time with that person, we come to understand what he or she likes and dislikes.

So it is with God. The more time we spend with Him, the more intimately we come to know Him. And the more intimately we come to know Him, the more we come to understand what He likes and dislikes. We come to understand, for example, that living in unrepentant sin is displeasing to Him while seeking righteousness brings Him great pleasure.

Relationships also involve communication. Can you imagine a newlywed husband and wife who never speak to one another? That wouldn't make sense. Where there is an intimate relationship, there is communication.

We communicate with God by prayer. We'll talk more about prayer a little later in the book. For now, it is enough to say that through prayer we talk to God, interact with Him, make requests of Him, verbalize our hurts and our joys to Him, and ask Him for help (Philippians 4:6). *And He hears us.*

The Christians in Bible times came to know and understand God in the ways mentioned above. They spent time with Him; they came to understand how He would respond under specific circumstances; and they communicated with Him. They had a relationship of intimacy with God—and this same kind of relationship is available to each of us through the person of Jesus Christ.

Since God is the same today as He was yesterday (Hebrews 13:8), how can we rest content unless we experience the same level of intimate communion with Him that the first-century believers had? How can we *not* be disturbed if our experience of knowing God falls woefully short of what the early Christians experienced?

The fact is, you and I today *can* enjoy a wonderfully intimate relationship with God. While Christ is not with us in the flesh, He *is* present with us spiritually. We may not see Him with our physical eyes, but He is here, seeking to walk with us side by side as a shepherd accompanies his sheep.

In a way, you and I have an advantage in coming to know Jesus Christ today because we have God's completed Word (the Bible). During New Testament times, the Gospels and epistles were not yet written and distributed. Hence, what the disciples and followers of Christ came to know was revealed to them gradually over a period of years, but you and I have all of God's Word available to us in the pages of Scripture. What a wonderful privilege we have!

The Blessing of Knowing God

The greatest blessing in life is that of coming to know God through the person of Jesus. To know Him and walk with Him—that is what brings true meaning to life.

As great as this blessing is, though, I would be remiss if I didn't also mention that knowing God brings with it many other blessings. For example, it is by knowing God that we can survive and thrive in this fallen world. The world can be a painful and disillusioning place to live in for people who do not know God. Forsake a relationship with God, and you sentence yourself to stumbling along the road of life blindfolded with no sense of direction and no genuine understanding of what surrounds you.[4]

There is certainly a great security in knowing God and walking with Him daily. It does me great good to get up each morning and remind myself that I am never out of Christ's mind. He loves me and He knows me—just like a friend (John 15:13-14). There is not a single moment that passes during the day that He takes His eyes off of me. His concern for me is perpetual. His attention is never distracted away from me. There is never a time when His tender care for my well-being falters. And so it is with all of God's children.

An Exclusive Relationship

There is no doubt that people in Bible times knew God intimately in their personal experience. In fact, knowing God was the main business among believers of ancient times.

We read that Enoch and Noah walked with God (Genesis 5:24; 6:9). God spoke to Noah (Genesis 6:13), to Abraham (Genesis 12:1), to Isaac (Genesis 26:24), to Jacob (Genesis 28:13), to Moses (Exodus 3:4), to Joshua (Joshua 1:1), to Gideon (Judges 6:25), to Samuel (1 Samuel 3:4), to David (1 Samuel 23:9-12), to Elijah (1 Kings 17:2-4), and to Isaiah (Isaiah 6:8). Likewise, in the New Testament God spoke to Peter, James, and John (Mark 9:7), to Philip (Acts 8:29), to Paul (Acts 9:4-6), and to Ananias (Acts 9:10).

The ancients also understood something that is very important for us to understand today: the *exclusive nature* of their relationship with God.

In the very first of the Ten Commandments, God said, "You shall have no other gods before me" (Exodus 20:3). God would permit no rival relationships with false gods or idols. Our relationship with the one true God must be supreme above all else in our lives.

Rejoice: For God Is Present

Where is God? While it is true that God dwells in heaven, He is also right here with us. He is everywhere-present. God is in the here and the now. He is spiritually with us every minute. C.S. Lewis, in his book *Letters to Malcolm*, said, "We may ignore, but we can nowhere evade, the presence of God. The world is crowded with Him. He walks everywhere *incognito*."[5]

We should not be surprised that our physical senses are incapable of perceiving the spiritual presence of God. In fact, there are many things we don't perceive. For example, a deer has a very keen sense of smell, and perceives odors we're not even aware of. The bat has a built-in radar system, enabling it to perceive all kinds of realities we don't perceive. Certain animals of the forest have night vision, which enables them to see things that we don't.

Just because we don't perceive some things with our physical senses doesn't mean those things don't exist. As I sit writing this book, radio waves from various radio stations are penetrating the walls of my house at an incredible rate. I can't physically perceive those radio waves. But I know they're there. All I have to do is turn on the radio, and those radio waves suddenly become undeniably present.

God is spiritually present with us, and He is spiritually perceived by those who have been spiritually "born again" (more on this later in the book). There is never a time when God is apart from us. And He seeks a personal relationship with us. He desires for us to desire Him.

Do you long to know God?

⟶ *A Verse to Hide in Your Heart* ⟵

"This is what the LORD *says:*
'Let not the wise man boast of his wisdom or the strong man
boast of his strength or the rich man boast of his riches,
but let him who boasts boast about this:
that he understands and knows me.'"

JEREMIAH 9:23-24

God is revealed *in* and *through* the person of Jesus Christ.

THREE

We Are Not Alone: God Reveals Himself

Isn't it wonderful that God didn't create man and then leave him to grope around in the dark trying to discover his Creator? God has always been the aggressor in making Himself known. He has always taken the initiative to reveal Himself to humankind. He does this through *revelation*.

When you think about it, revelation makes good sense when you consider that God is our Father. No loving parent would ever deliberately keep out of his or her child's sight so that the child grew up without knowing of the parent's existence. That would be the height of cruelty. Likewise, for God to create us and then not communicate with us would not be in character for a loving heavenly Father.

The word *communication* brings to mind someone coming to us to tell us about himself—telling us what he knows, opening up his mind to us, asking for our attention, and seeking a response.[1] That is what divine revelation is all about. God has come to us to tell us about Himself, tell us what He knows, open His mind to us, ask for our attention, and seek a response from us.

Now, there are two primary ways that God has revealed Himself—through *general* revelation and *special* revelation. Let's take a brief look at both of these.

General Revelation

General revelation refers to revelation that is available to *all persons* of *all times*. An example of this would be God's revelation of Himself in the world of nature (Psalm 19).

By observing nature, we can detect something of God's existence, and discern something of His divine power and glory. We might say that the whole world is God's "kindergarten" to teach us the ABCs of the reality of God. And since Jesus Christ is the one who created the physical universe (Colossians 1:16), the revelation of God in the universe is Christ's doing.

The great French theologian John Calvin once said, "Men cannot open their eyes without being compelled to see God. Upon his individual works he has engraved unmistakable marks of his glory. This skillful ordering of the universe is for us a sort of mirror in which we can contemplate God, who is otherwise invisible."[2]

Of course, there are limitations to how much we can learn from general revelation. For example, general revelation does not tell us anything about God's cure for man's sin problem. It doesn't tell us about the "gospel message." (These kinds of things require *special* revelation.) But general revelation does give us enough information about God's existence that if we reject it and refuse to turn to God, then God is justified in bringing condemnation against us (Romans 1:20).

Special Revelation

Special revelation refers to God's specific and clear revelation via His mighty acts in history, the person of Jesus Christ, and His message spoken through Old Testament prophets (like Isaiah and Daniel) and New Testament apostles (like Paul and Peter). Let's take a brief look at each of these.

God's Revelation in History

If there really is a personal God who created humankind, then we would naturally expect that He would reveal Himself among us in the outworking of human history. And indeed, God *has* manifest Himself historically.

God is the *living* God, and He has communicated knowledge of Himself through the ebb and flow of historical experience. The Bible is first and foremost a record of God's interactions with Abraham, Isaac, Jacob, the twelve tribes of Israel, the apostle Paul, Peter, John, and many others in biblical times.

The greatest revelatory act of God in the Old Testament was the deliverance of Israel from bondage in Egypt. God, through Moses, inflicted ten plagues on the Egyptians—plagues that showed His awesome power (Exodus 7–12). God's demonstration of His power was all the more impressive because the Egyptians believed their many false gods could protect them from such plagues.

It's important to note that the historical miracles and events wrought by God were always accompanied by spoken words. A miracle or event was never left to speak for itself. Nor were people left to infer whatever conclusions they wanted to draw from the event. God made sure that when a significant event occurred there was a prophet on hand to interpret it.

For example, Moses was present to record everything related to the Exodus. Jeremiah and Ezekiel were on hand to record all that happened during Israel's time of exile. Isaiah was present to preserve a record of the Israelites' return from exile. And the apostles testified about everything related to the life and death of Jesus. Over a period of many centuries, then, God has revealed Himself and He always made sure that His actions were adequately recorded!

Here's an important fact we should pay close attention to. In 1 Peter 1:10-11 we are told that it was the Spirit of Christ who spoke through the mouths of all the prophets who wrote the Bible. That means that the revelation that came through the prophets *was Christ's doing!* From the very beginning, Christ has been providing revelation about God (John 1:9).

God's Ultimate Revelation in Jesus Christ

The only way for God to be able to fully do and say all that He wanted was to leave His eternal residence and enter the arena of humanity. This He did in the person of Jesus Christ. Jesus was Immanuel—"God with us." He was God's ultimate "special" revelation.

Why was it so necessary for Jesus to come as God's fullest revelation? Because God is a Spirit. And because He is a Spirit, He is invisible. With our normal senses, we can't perceive Him, other than what we can detect in general revelation.

Not only that, man is also spiritually blind and deaf. Since the fall of man in the Garden of Eden, man has lacked true spiritual perception. So humankind was in need of special revelation from God in the worst sort of way.

Jesus—as eternal God—took on human flesh so He could be God's fullest revelation to man (Hebrews 1:2-3). Jesus was a revelation of God not just in His person (as God) but in His life and teachings as well. By observing the things Jesus did and the things Jesus said, we learn a great deal about God. For example:

- God's awesome power was revealed in Jesus (John 3:2).

- God's incredible wisdom was revealed in Jesus (1 Corinthians 1:24).

- God's boundless love was revealed and demonstrated by Jesus (1 John 3:16).

- God's unfathomable grace was revealed in Jesus (2 Thessalonians 1:12).

These verses serve as the backdrop as to why Jesus told a group of Pharisees, "When a man believes in me, he does not believe in me only, but in the one who sent me" (John 12:44). Jesus likewise told His disciple Philip that "anyone who has seen me has seen the Father" (John 14:9). *Jesus was the ultimate revelation of God!*

God's Revelation in the Bible

Another key means of special revelation is the Bible. In this one book, God has provided everything He wants us to know about Him and how we can have a relationship with Him.

God is the one who caused the Bible to be written. And through it He speaks to us today just as He spoke to people in ancient times when those words were first given. The Bible is to be received as *God's words to us* and revered and obeyed as such. As we submit to the Bible's authority, we place ourselves under the authority of the living God.

The Scriptures "are God preaching, God talking, God telling, God instructing, God setting before us the right way to think and speak about him. The Scriptures are God showing us himself: God communicating to us who he is and what he has done so that in the response of faith we may truly know him and live our lives in fellowship with him."[3]

In a way the Bible functions as an eyeglass. It enables us to see God clearly. Without the eyeglass, we don't see clearly. We see only a blurred reality. But with the eyeglass, all comes into clear focus. We see God as He really is.[4]

The Inspiration of the Bible

It is truly amazing to contemplate that the Bible's authors were from all walks of life—kings, peasants, philosophers, fishermen, physicians, statesmen, scholars, poets, and farmers. These individuals lived in different cultures, had vastly different experiences, and often were quite different in character. Yet in spite of these differences, the Bible has a remarkable continuity that can be observed from Genesis to Revelation.

How could this be? How did God accomplish this? It's related to a process we call *inspiration*.

Biblical inspiration may be defined as God's superintending of the human authors so that, using their own individual personalities (and even their writing styles), they composed and recorded without error His revelation to man. Because of inspiration, we can rest assured that what the human authors wrote was precisely what God wanted written.

The word *inspiration* literally means "God-breathed." And because Scripture is breathed out by God, it is true and has no errors. We could put this in the form of a logical argument: The first premise of our argument is that *God is true* (Romans 3:4). The second premise is that *God breathed out the Scriptures* (2 Timothy 3:16). Our conclusion, then, is simple: *Therefore, the Scriptures are true* (John 17:17).[5]

The Holy Spirit's Role in Inspiration

Second Peter 1:21 tells us that "prophecy never had its origin in the will of man, but men spoke from God as they were carried along by the Holy Spirit." The phrase "carried along" in this verse literally means to be "borne along."

Even though human beings—God's prophets—were used in the process of writing down God's Word, they were all literally "borne along" by the Holy Spirit. This means the authors were not the originators of God's message. Rather, "God *moved* and the prophet *mouthed* these truths; God *revealed* and man *recorded* His word."[6]

Interestingly, the Greek word for "moved" in 2 Peter 1:21 is the same word found in Acts 27:15-17. In that passage, we read about a group of experienced sailors who could not navigate their ship because the wind was so strong. The ship was being driven, directed, and carried about by the wind. This is similar to the Spirit's driving, directing, and carrying the human authors of the Bible as He wished. So the word "moved" in 2 Peter 1:21 is a strong word, indicating the Spirit's complete superintendence over the human authors. Yet, just as the sailors were active on the ship (though the wind, not the sailors, actually controlled the ship's movement), so also were the human authors active in writing as the Spirit directed.

As a direct result of the Holy Spirit's superintendence over the human authors, the Scriptures are inerrant. Bible scholar Edward J. Young, in his book *Thy Word Is Truth*, explains inerrancy this way: "The Scriptures possess the quality of freedom from error. They are exempt from the liability to make mistakes, and are incapable of error. In all their teachings they are in perfect accord with the truth."[7]

Fulfilled Prophecy: A Proof of Divine Inspiration

From the book of Genesis to the book of Malachi, the Old Testament abounds with anticipations of the coming Messiah. Numerous predictions made hundreds of years before the actual event—fulfilled to the "crossing of the t" and the "dotting of the i"—relate to His birth, life, ministry, death, resurrection, and glory. These fulfilled prophecies constitute a powerful proof for the inspiration of Scripture.

There are many examples we could point to. Let me just mention a few. We are told that the Messiah would be born of a virgin (Isaiah 7:14). We are also told He would be born from the line of Abraham (Genesis 12) *and* from the line of David (2 Samuel 7:14-29). He would be born in Bethlehem (Micah 5:2). (Notice that Jesus couldn't possibly have conspired to fulfill these prophecies regarding His lineage and birth.) Jesus would also suffer and bear the sins of humanity (Isaiah 53). These and virtually hundreds of other prophecies were fulfilled *literally* in the person of Jesus Christ.

It is only logical to conclude that if these prophecies were written many hundreds of years before they were fulfilled—and if *all* of these prophecies were, in fact, *precisely* fulfilled—then clearly the Scriptures are divine in origin and not manmade.

The Divine Authority of the Bible

Since the written revelation from God has been recorded under the Spirit's superintendence and is "the very breath of God," the Bible is therefore authoritative—just as authoritative as God Himself. The authority of Scripture cannot be separated from the authority of God.

This means that what the Bible affirms (or denies), it affirms (or denies) with the very authority of God.[8] For this reason, theologian John Calvin said, "We owe to Scripture the same reverence which we owe to God."[9]

The Bible: A Jesus Book

Any objective student of Scripture must inevitably come to the conclusion that the Bible is a Jesus book. From beginning to end, Jesus is the focal point of God's Word.

Jesus once told some Jews, "You diligently study the Scriptures because you think that by them you possess eternal life. These are the Scriptures that testify about me, yet you refuse to come to me to have life" (John 5:39-40). The Jews to whom Jesus spoke knew the shell of the Bible but were neglecting the kernel within it. It is not the Book that saves, but the Savior of the Book.

Jesus affirmed that the Scriptures were "concerning himself" (Luke 24:27), were "written about me" (verse 44), were "written of me" (Hebrews 10:7 NASB), and "bear witness to me" (John 5:39 NASB). The Bible is indeed a Jesus book.

Jesus: The Heart of Divine Revelation

What can we conclude in this chapter?

• Because Jesus is the one who created the universe, the revelation of God in the universe is His doing.

• Because it was the Spirit of Christ who spoke through the mouths of the prophets (1 Peter 1:11), the revelation that came through the prophets was His doing.

• Jesus Himself is the ultimate revelation of God—not just in His person (as God), but in His life and teachings as well.

• God has given us special revelation in the Bible, which is most definitely a Jesus book.

It seems clear that in a very general way Jesus has taken it upon Himself to reveal God to us. Whether through the creation, the prophets, or directly through Himself, Jesus has revealed God to us.

The question now is, What will you do with this revelation of God? *How will you respond to what Jesus has made known to you?*

⟿ *A Verse to Hide in Your Heart* ⟿

"In the past God spoke to our forefathers
through the prophets at many times and in various ways,
but in these last days he has spoken to us by his Son,
whom he appointed heir of all things,
and through whom he made the universe."

HEBREWS 1:1-2

> The God that Jesus came to reveal (God the
> Father) is awesome in power and perfect in
> every way.

FOUR

Behold Your God!

B elief in some kind of God is fairly universal. Whatever period of history
scholars study—whatever culture they
examine—they find people acknowledging some kind of
deity.

During the past two centuries archaeologists have
unearthed the ruins of many ancient civilizations. None has
ever been found that did not yield some evidence of belief in
a god (or a group of gods). Human beings have worshiped
the sun, carved idols, animals, objects, and even other
human beings (such as the emperors of ancient Rome).

Some people have given up the pursuit of God in frus-
tration, calling themselves atheists or agnostics. But they
find it necessary to fill the vacuum left within them with
some other kind of deity (or god). Such people make up
their own "god"—money, work, success, fame, recreation,
sex, alcohol, or even food.

Jesus Reveals the True God

As we have noted in previous chapters, Jesus came into the world to reveal the one true God to humanity (John 1:18). Jesus was the ultimate revelation of God to man—a fact Jesus Himself often emphasized to the people He encountered. Jesus emphatically declared, for example, that "anyone who has seen me has seen [God] the Father" (John 14:9, insert added).

Who is this "one true God" that Jesus came to reveal? The question is an important one. As we noted in chapter 2, which is titled "Knowing God: The Highest Priority," the main business of our lives should be getting to know God.

Of course, Jesus' declaration that "anyone who has seen me has seen the Father" ultimately means that getting to know Jesus is essentially the same as getting to know God the Father. Jesus *is* God. And that's why He's the perfect revelation of God. Jesus, as eternal God (*the second person of the Trinity*), stepped out of heaven and became a man on earth in order to reveal God the Father (*the first person of the Trinity*). (If this is difficult for you to understand, don't worry; we'll talk more about the Trinity later in the chapter.)

Only One True God

There is only one true God. That must be our starting point. There are no other gods besides the one true God of Scripture.

Way back during the time of Moses, God affirmed, "See now that I myself am He! There is no god besides me" (Deuteronomy 32:39). The God of the Bible is without rival.

We find the same truth emphasized in Isaiah 44:6: "This is what the LORD says—Israel's King and Redeemer, the LORD Almighty: I am the first and I am the last; apart from me there is no God." Isaiah 46:9 likewise quotes God as saying, "I am God, and there is no other; I am God, and there is none like me."

The Only True God Is a Person

A person is a conscious being—someone who thinks, feels, and purposes, and carries these purposes into action. A person engages in active relationships with other people. You can talk to a person and get a response. You can share feelings and ideas with him. You can argue with him, love him, and even hate him.

Surely by this definition God must be understood as a person. After all, God is a conscious being who thinks, feels, and purposes—and He carries these purposes into action. He engages in relationships with others. You can talk to God and get a response from Him.

The biblical picture of God is that of a loving personal Father unto whom believers may cry, "Abba" (Romans 8:15). "Abba" is an Aramaic term of great intimacy, loosely meaning "daddy."

Jesus often spoke of God as a loving Father. Indeed, God is the "father of compassion" who comforts all believers (2 Corinthians 1:3). He is often portrayed in Scripture as compassionately responding to the personal request of His people. (A few good examples may be found in Exodus 3:7-8, Job 34:28, Psalm 81:10, 91:14-15, 2 Corinthians 1:3-4, and Philippians 4:6-7.)

God Is a Spirit

The Scriptures tell us that God is Spirit (John 4:24). And a spirit does not have flesh and bones (Luke 24:39). Hence, it is wrong to think of God as a physical being. (At the same time, of course, we need to keep in mind that when Jesus became a man in order to reveal God, He took on human flesh. So, Jesus—from the moment He became a man—*did* have a physical body.)

Because God is a spirit, He is invisible. He cannot be seen. First Timothy 1:17 refers to God as "the King eternal, immortal, invisible, the only God." Colossians 1:15 speaks of "the invisible God." John 1:18 tells us, "No one has ever seen God [the Father], but God the One and Only [Jesus Christ], who is at the Father's side, has made him known [when Jesus took on human flesh and became a man]" (inserts added). When Jesus became a man, He became a *visible* revelation of the *invisible* God.

If God is a Spirit, then how are we to interpret the many references in Scripture to God's face, ears, eyes, hands, strong arm, and so on? The ancients often described God metaphorically in humanlike language because they considered Him very much alive and active in human affairs. To the men and women of the Old Testament God was real. They knew Him as a person. And the clearest, most succinct way they could express their view of God and their interaction with Him was in the language of human personality and activity—not in cold metaphysical jargon.

Such language, however, is not to be taken in a woodenly literal sense. When Moses spoke to God "face to face" (Exodus 33:11), this doesn't mean Moses saw a divine face with eyes, ears, a nose, and a mouth. Rather it means that Moses spoke to God *in His direct presence* and *in an intimate way*.

There are other examples of metaphorical language used of God in the Bible. For example, Psalm 91:4 says, "He will cover you with his feathers, and under his wings you will find refuge." Are we to take this literally, envisioning God as sort of a giant bird with wings and feathers? Of course not. This is simply metaphorical language intended to communicate spiritual truth.

The Living God

As we scan through the Bible we cannot help but notice how often the God of Scripture is referred to as "the living God" (Deuteronomy 5:26; 1 Samuel 17:26-36; Psalm 84:2). The living God is truly "among" His people (Joshua 3:10).

This is illustrated in the life of the Old Testament prophet Daniel. Daniel was thrown into a lion's den and was forced to stay there the entire night. The next morning, the king—who was sympathetic toward Daniel—ran to the den and shouted, "Daniel, servant of the living God, has your God, whom you serve continually, been able to rescue you from the lions?" Daniel affirmed that yes indeed, the living God had rescued him. The king quickly had Daniel removed from the den and issued a decree that all the people in his kingdom must fear and reverence the God of Daniel, for He is "the living God" who endures forever and who performs signs and wonders (Daniel 6:19-27).

In his wonderful book *The Living God*, Bible scholar R.T. France explains how the ancients viewed God:

> Watch the hand of this living God intervening, in answer to His people's prayers, working miracles, converting thousands, opening prison doors, and raising the dead, guiding His messengers to people and places they had never thought of, supervising the whole operation and every figure in it so as to work out His purpose in the end. Is it any wonder they prayed, constantly, not in vague generalities, but in daring specific requests? To them, God was real; to them He was the living God.[1]

God's Names

In the ancient world, a name was not a mere label as it is today. A name was considered to reveal certain characteristics about the person. Indeed, knowing a person's name amounted to knowing his essence.

We see this illustrated in the names of major Bible characters. The name *Abraham*, for instance, means "father of a multitude," and was quite fitting since Abraham was the father of the Jewish nation. The name *David* means "beloved," and was appropriate because David was a king specially loved by God. The name *Solomon* comes from a word meaning "peace," and is fitting because Solomon's reign was characterized by peace. In each case, we learn something about the individual from his name.

In the same way, we learn much about God from the names ascribed to Him in the Bible. These names are not man-made; God Himself used these names to describe Himself. They are *characteristic* names, each one making known something new about Him. Here are just a few of the names used of God in Scripture:

God is El Shaddai. *El* in Hebrew refers to "Mighty God." But *Shaddai* qualifies this meaning and adds something to it (Genesis 17:1-20). Many scholars believe *Shaddai* is derived from a root word that refers to a mother's breast. This name, then, indicates not only that God is a Mighty God, but that He is full of compassion, grace, and mercy. This is a tender name of God. Our Mighty God and Creator is to His children what a loving mother is to her dependent infant. He sustains and nurtures us.

God is Jehovah-Nissi (meaning "the Lord Our Banner"). Israel could not defeat her enemies in her own strength. She was weak in the face of her mighty foes. But the battles were to be the Lord's because He was Israel's banner—her source of victory (Exodus 17:15).

This name associates God with warfare on behalf of His people. God wants us to know that He is the one who fights our battles.

Do you feel defeated? Take heart. Turn to God and let Him fight your battles.

God is the Lord of Hosts. God is often called the "Lord of hosts" in the Bible. This title pictures God as the sovereign commander of a great heavenly army of angels (Psalm 89:6,8). It should give every Christian a supreme sense of security to know that this heavenly army of angels—headed by God, the Lord of hosts—is committed to watching over us.

There are many other names used of God in Scripture. For example, God is *our rock* (Deuteronomy 32:4-31). This points to God's strength and power. God is called *our fortress* (Psalm 18:2). This speaks of the protection God provides us. God is called *our shield* (Genesis 15:1). This points to God as our daily defense. God is also called *our strength* (Psalm 81:1). This points to how God infuses us with His power so we can face any circumstance.

The Perfections of God

When we talk about God's perfections, we're talking about His attributes or characteristics. Understanding God's perfections not only helps us to know Him better, it also helps us see more clearly how God relates to us in our personal relationship with Him—especially in regard to how He takes care of us. Below we will consider a few of God's perfections and the ramifications they have for believers.

God Is Eternal

God, as an eternal being, has always existed. He never came into being at a point in time. He is beyond time altogether. God is the King eternal (1 Timothy 1:17) who alone is immortal (6:16).

A comforting ramification of God's eternal nature is the absolute confidence that He will never cease to exist. He will always be there for us. His continued providential control of our lives is thereby assured.

God Is Love

God isn't just characterized by love. He is the very *personification* of love (1 John 4:8). Love virtually permeates

His being. And God's love is not dependent upon the lovability of the object (human beings). God loves us despite the fact that we are fallen in sin (John 3:16). God loves the *sinner*, though He hates the *sin*.

This is important for us to remember, especially during those times when we're acutely aware of our failures. Sometimes we may find ourselves on a guilt trip and we feel unworthy of God's love. In fact, we might feel like worms before God. But this feeling is not rooted in God's actual feelings toward us. *He loves us even when we are unlovable.*

God Is Everywhere-Present

The Scriptures tell us that God is everywhere-present (Psalm 139:7-8). How comforting to know that no matter where we go, we will never escape the presence of our beloved God. Because He is everywhere-present, we can be confident of His real presence at all times. Just as a good shepherd never leaves his sheep, so does God never leave His children alone. He is with us always. We will always know the blessing of walking with Him in every trial and circumstance of life.

God Is All-Knowing

Because God is all-knowing, He does not learn. He knows all things, both actual and possible (Matthew 11:21-23). He knows all things past (Isaiah 41:22), present (Hebrews 4:13), and future (Isaiah 46:10). And because He knows all things, there can be no increase or decrease in His knowledge. Psalm 147:5 affirms that God's understanding "has no limit."

One of the great things about God being all-knowing is that He can never discover anything in our lives that will cause Him to change His mind about us being in His family. When we become Christians, God is fully aware of every sin we have ever committed and will ever commit in the future. That God knows everything about us and *accepts us anyway* should give every child of God a profound sense of security.

A.W. Tozer said it well: "No talebearer can inform on us, no enemy can make an accusation stick; no forgotten skeleton can come tumbling out of some hidden closet to abash us and expose our past; no unsuspected weakness in our characters can come to light to turn God away from us, since He knew us utterly before we knew Him and called us to Himself in the full knowledge of everything that was against us."[2]

God's all-knowingness also has ramifications regarding tragedies that occur in our lives. When life throws us a punch, we can rest in the knowledge that God has known about it from the beginning of time and is working things out for His glory and for our ultimate good (Romans 8:28).

God Is All-Powerful

God is portrayed in Scripture as being all-powerful (Jeremiah 32:17). There are many practical ramifications regarding God's unlimited power. Not only does He have the power to fulfill all the promises He has made to us in Scripture, but also He has the power to see believers securely into heaven without a single one falling away. Moreover, the same awesome power that raised Jesus from the dead will one day raise us from the dead. We may rest serenely in the knowledge that all is in the hands of our all-powerful God.

God Is Sovereign

God is sovereign in the sense that He rules the universe, controls all things, and is Lord over all (Ephesians 1). There is nothing that can happen in this universe that is beyond the reach of His control.

It should bring supreme peace to every believing soul to know that God is sovereignly overseeing all that comes into our lives. No matter what we may encounter, and no matter how much we may fail to understand why certain things happen in life, the knowledge that our sovereign God is in control is like a firm anchor in the midst of life's storms.

God Is Holy

God's holiness means not just that He is entirely separate from all evil but also that He is absolutely righteous (Leviticus 19:2). He is pure in every way.

A key ramification of this is that if we want to fellowship with God, we have to take personal holiness seriously. Walking daily with God in fellowship involves living in a way that is pleasing to Him.

God Is Just

That God is just means that He carries out His righteous standards justly and with equity. There is never any partiality or unfairness in God's dealings with people (Zephaniah 3:5; Romans 3:26).

The fact that God is just is both a comfort and a warning. It is a comfort for those who have been wronged in life. They can rest assured that God will right all wrongs in the end. It is a warning for those who think they have been getting away with evil. Justice will prevail in the end!

God Is a Trinity

Earlier in the chapter I mentioned the doctrine of the Trinity. This is unquestionably one of the most difficult Bible doctrines to understand. I won't mince words here; this is a hard one.

I need to emphasize, however, that for us to be able to understand everything about God—including the doctrine of the Trinity—we'd have to have the very mind of God. Only a mind as great as God's could understand all there is to know about God.

This brings me to share a story involving the great theologian Augustine. One day while walking along the beach he was puzzling over the doctrine of the Trinity. On the beach he observed a young boy with a bucket, running back and forth to pour water into a little hole. Augustine asked, "What are you doing?"

The boy replied, "I'm trying to put the ocean into this hole."

Augustine smiled, recognizing the utter futility of what the boy was attempting to do.

After pondering the boy's words for a few moments, however, Augustine came to a sudden realization. He realized that he had been trying to put an infinite God into his finite mind. It can't be done.[3]

We can accept God's revelation to us that He is triune in nature and that He has infinite perfections. But with our finite minds we cannot fully understand everything about God. *Our God is an awesome God!*

The doctrine of the Trinity states that there is only one God, but in the unity of the Godhead there are three co-equal and co-eternal persons—the Father, the Son, and the Holy Spirit. This doctrine is based on three lines of evidence in Scripture: 1) evidence that there is only one true God; 2) evidence that there are three persons who are God; and 3) evidence that indicates three-in-oneness within the Godhead.

Space forbids a detailed treatment of this doctrine, but the following brief summary is sufficient to show that it is a biblical doctrine.

There Is One True God

As we seek to explore what Scripture says about the mystery of the Trinity, we begin with the recognition that in the course of God's self-disclosure to humankind, He revealed His nature to man in progressive stages. First, God revealed His essential unity and uniqueness—that is, He revealed that He is *one* and that He is the *only true* God.

This was a necessary starting point for God's self-revelation. Throughout history Israel was surrounded by pagan nations deeply engulfed in the belief that there are many gods. Through the prophets, God communicated and affirmed to Israel that there is only one true God (Deuteronomy 6:4).

Three Persons Who Are Called God

As history unfolded, God progressively revealed more and more about Himself until man finally came to see that while there is only one God, there are three distinct persons within the Godhead. Each of these three persons is called God in Scripture: the Father (1 Peter 1:2), the Son (John 20:28), and the Holy Spirit (Acts 5:3-4).

Moreover, each of the three persons possess the attributes of deity. For example, all three are *everywhere-present* (Matthew 19:26; 28:20; Psalm 139:7). All three are *all-knowing* (Romans 11:33; Matthew 9:4; 1 Corinthians 2:10). And all three are *all-powerful* (1 Peter 1:5; Matthew 28:18; Romans 15:19).

Three-In-Oneness in the Godhead

So far we've seen that 1) there is only one true God, and 2) the Father, Son, and Holy Spirit are called God in Scripture. We also find three-in-oneness emphasized in Scripture.

For example, just prior to His return to heaven, Jesus told the disciples, "Go and make disciples of all nations, baptizing them in the *name* of the Father and of the Son and of the Holy Spirit" (Matthew 28:19). The word "name" is singular in the Greek, indicating that there is one God. But there are three distinct persons within the Godhead— the Father, the Son, and the Holy Spirit.

As well, at the close of Paul's second letter to the church at Corinth, he said, "May the grace of the Lord Jesus Christ, and the love of God [the Father], and the fellowship of the Holy Spirit be with you all" (2 Corinthians 13:14, insert added).

Considering all the above verses together, we must come to the conclusion that there is *one God* but there are *three persons* within the Godhead.

Finite minds will never be able to fully grasp how three persons can be in one God. However, like Augustine, we must remember that finite minds cannot fully understand an infinite God. What we *can* do is to anchor our faith on what Scripture reveals to be true: *God is a Trinity.*

We can certainly take comfort in the realization that all three persons of the Trinity are actively involved in ministering to us. For example, the Father keeps us securely in His hands in terms of our salvation (John 10:29). Jesus prays for us (Hebrews 7:25) and guides us as a shepherd guides his sheep (John 10:1-18). The Holy Spirit is our divine helper and comforter (John 14:16) and helps us to understand the meaning of Scripture (1 Corinthians 2:12). *Praise be to the triune God!*

—⧖— *A Verse to Hide in Your Heart* —⧖—

"How awesome is the LORD Most High,
the great King over all the earth."

PSALM 47:2

> Sin severs our personal relationship with the
> Lord.

FIVE

From Creation to Corruption: Man's Sin

I n our day it is popular to deny that there is any such thing as sin. Many people think sin is an outdated concept.

When you think about it, though, this denial doesn't seem reasonable. Suppose a medical doctor were to say that disease is an outdated concept. Despite the fact that there is widespread evidence for disease—with people suffering all kinds of deadly illnesses—the doctor still says there is no disease. You would think he was a madman, right?

Such a doctor would do you very little good. After all, if you got sick, he wouldn't be able to help you because he wouldn't accurately diagnose your problem.

In the same way, there are people today who say there is no sin, even though the evidence for sin is everywhere around us. A helpful exercise in this regard is to read the morning newspaper. Here we will find overwhelming evidence to confirm the rampant mess that human beings have made in this world.

Of course, if people do not recognize a sin problem, they will never seek the cure for their spiritual ills—Jesus Christ, the Savior. A weak view of sin always produces a weak view of salvation. A weak view of sin blinds a person to the need for a Savior.

Now, some people may respond, "Well, we may have a sin problem, but it's not very serious. We can overcome our weaknesses." But is that an accurate statement? I hardly think so.

Let us suppose, for illustration purposes, that each of us commits an average of three "little" sins per day. That adds up to 21 sins per week, 84 sins per month, 1,092 sins per year, or 76,440 sins over a lifetime (assuming we live to age 70). That's a pretty serious sin problem. And who among us would dare claim that we are guilty of only three "little" sins per day?

Let us be clear on this: The only way to have an accurate cure is to have an accurate diagnosis. God diagnoses man as having a serious sin problem—and the cure is believing in Jesus Christ for salvation.

The Beginning of Sin: Satan's Rebellion

Where did sin come from? What is sin's origin? How did it arise?

The beginning of sin in the universe is actually rooted not in man but in a great angelic personage known as Lucifer (whose name changed to Satan after his sin against God). Scripture indicates that Lucifer was created as an incredibly beautiful and powerful angel. And he became so impressed with his beauty and power that he wanted to take God's place.

First Timothy 3:6 tells us that Lucifer's sin was that of pride. In Isaiah 14:13-14 we read that Lucifer, in his pride, wanted to exercise the authority and control in this world that rightfully belongs to God alone. His sin was a direct challenge to the power and authority of God.

Lucifer's sin against God was especially wicked for four reasons.

- There was no previous example of sin in the universe. Lucifer was the first to fall.

- Lucifer was originally created by God in a state of beauty and perfection. He had everything going for him. But he corrupted himself.

- Lucifer had incredibly great intelligence. He was certainly aware that there would be consequences for rebelling against the Creator.

- Lucifer enjoyed perfect fellowship with the Creator. Despite living in such a perfect environment, Lucifer rebelled against the One who brought him into existence.

Lucifer's sin, of course, had widespread effects. It had a negative effect on other angels (Revelation 12:7-9) and on people everywhere (Ephesians 2:2). It positioned him as the diabolical ruler of this world (John 16:11). And it negatively affected all the nations of the world, for he works to deceive them (Revelation 20:3).

As a result of this heinous sin against God, Lucifer was banished from living in heaven (Isaiah 14:12). He became corrupt, and his name changed from *Lucifer* ("morning star") to *Satan* ("adversary"). His power became completely perverted (Isaiah 14:12-17). His purpose in life became that of standing against God and all who are related to God. Ultimately, he will be thrown into the Lake of Fire, where he will suffer forever (Matthew 25:41).

The Creation of Man

When God created man, He made him from the dust of the ground and breathed the breath of life into him

(Genesis 2:4-7). How awesome a moment that must have been! At one moment no man existed; the next moment, there he stood.

Man was created in the "image of God" (Genesis 1:26-27). Scripture indicates that man was created in God's image in the sense that he is a finite reflection of God in his rational nature (Colossians 3:10), his moral nature (Ephesians 4:24), and his dominion over creation (Genesis 1:27-28). In the same way that the moon reflects the brilliant light of the sun, so also is finite man—as created in God's image—a reflection of God in these aspects.

Another key aspect of man being created in the image of God is that man is a relational creature. God made man as a social being. God specially endowed man with a capacity to relate to other people, just as God Himself has that capacity.

After God created Adam and Eve, He immediately initiated a personal relationship with them (you can read about this in Genesis 1–3). Unfortunately, Adam and Eve ended up severing that relationship. They sinned against God. The creature rebelled against the Creator.

Adam and Eve's Sin

One would think that such a noble creature as man would do no wrong. But soon after their creation, Adam and Eve sinned against God and catapulted the entire human race into sin. The serpent (Satan)—who had previously fallen into prideful sin—sneaked up to Eve, and in a fatal conversation, he led her astray. He tempted her and she gave in to the temptation. Sin was then conceived in humanity (Genesis 3:1-7).

When Adam and Eve sinned, they broke their relationship and fellowship with God, and a nature of sin and rebellion against God was introduced into them and *through* them into all their descendants (Romans 5:12). This nature is the source of all our individual "acts" of sin and is the major reason why we are rendered unacceptable for a relationship with a holy God.

The idea that *all* human beings are born in sin is emphasized in Romans 5:19: "Through the disobedience of the one man the many were made sinners." In keeping with this, 1 Corinthians 15:21-22 tells us that "death came through a man" and "in Adam all die."

In Psalm 51:5 King David said, "Surely I was sinful at birth, sinful from the time my mother conceived me." According to this verse, we are born into the world in a state of sin. The sin nature is passed on from conception. This is why Ephesians 2:3 says we are *"by nature objects of wrath"* (emphasis added).

Adam's own initial sin, then, caused him to fall, and in the Fall he became an entirely different being from a moral standpoint. Every child of Adam is born with the Adamic nature and is always prone to sin. It remains an active force in every Christian's life. It is never said to be removed or eradicated in this life (Romans 8:4; Galatians 5:16-17).

Now, when Adam and Eve sinned, they immediately sensed an alienation from God and even went so far as to try to hide themselves from Him (Genesis 3:8). They sinned and, in their panic, frantically tried to do the impossible: They tried to withdraw and avoid having to face God altogether.

You and I are the same way. We often sense that we have let God down, and in our attitude and actions we tend to try to hide from Him in shame. This sense of separation from God and the accompanying shame is one of the worst results of man's sin problem.

We are born into this world with our back to God. As a result of the Fall, it is now human nature to do over and over again what Adam and Eve attempted to do in Genesis 3. That is, we sin and then we try to hide from God so that we don't have to face our guilt. *What futility!*

The Penalty for Sin: Death

When Adam and Eve sinned, they passed immediately into a state of spiritual death, meaning that they were spiritually separated from God. They were kicked out of the Garden of Eden and a sword-bearing angel was posted to guard it.

The penalty for sin, though, includes both spiritual *and* physical death (Romans 6:23; 7:13). Death, in the biblical sense, literally means "separation." Spiritual death, then, is spiritual separation from God. Physical death is separation of the soul from the body. Physical death is the inevitable result of spiritual death. The fall into sin introduced the process of age and decay, leading ultimately to death—the separation of the soul from the body.

Adam and Eve's expulsion from the Garden of Eden gave geographical expression to humankind's spiritual separation from God—our unfitness to stand before Him and enjoy the intimacy of His presence (Genesis 3:23). Because of our sin, God's presence becomes a place of dread. The fiery sword of the guarding angel—which barred the way back to Eden—represents the terrible truth that in his sin man is separated from God (Romans 1:18).

In Scripture, then, there is a direct connection between sin and death (Romans 5:12). One causes the other. Death came into the universe because of sin.

This means that death—and separation from God—is not natural. It is an unnatural intruder. God intended for people to live and have fellowship with Him. Death is therefore foreign and hostile to human life. Death has arisen because of our rebellion against God. It is a form of God's judgment.

But in a way there is grace even in physical death. For physical death, as a judgment against sin, serves to prevent us from living forever in a state of sin. When Adam and Eve sinned in the Garden of Eden (Genesis 2:17; 3:19), God assigned an angel to guard the Tree of Life. This was to protect against Adam and Eve eating the Tree of Life while they were yet in a body of sin. How horrible it would be to live eternally in such a state!

Today man still sins, still defies authority, and still acts independently of God. A great gulf exists between sinful man and God (Isaiah 59:2). Twentieth-century men and women are no different from Adam and Eve. We may have created some sophisticated technology, built a few sky-scrapers, and written millions of books. But there is still a chasm between sinful man and a holy God.

Today we still struggle with a sense of separation from God. Each of us is born into this world in a state of spiritual death; therefore, each of us is born in a state of separation from God. Our sins blot out God's face from us as effectively as the clouds do the sun. Until our sins are forgiven, we are exiles, far from our true home. We have no communion with God.

It is impossible for God to receive into His presence people who do not measure up to His perfect character. In 1 John 1:5 we read, "This is the message we have heard from him and declare to you: God is light; in him there is no darkness at all." God, who is light, cannot fellowship with the darkness of human sin. Man's sin put a barrier—a wide chasm—between him and God.

Missing the Target

A key meaning of sin in the Bible is "to miss the target." Sin is the failure to live up to God's standards. *All* of us miss the target. There is not one person who is capable of fulfilling all of God's laws at all times (Romans 3:23).

We might illustrate this in the following way. Let's say we're going to have a contest to see who can throw a rock to the moon. I'm sure that a muscle-bound athlete would be able to throw a rock much further than I could—but not even the most muscular athlete in the world is capable of throwing a rock to the moon. All of us fall short; all of us miss the target.

In the same way, there may be some people who are more righteous than others. But all of us fall short of God's infinitely perfect standards. No one can measure up to His perfection.

In the presence of God's holiness—His "light"—the dirt of sin shows up crystal clear. Remember what happened to the prophet Isaiah? Here was a relatively righteous man. But when Isaiah beheld God in His infinite holiness, the prophet's own sin came into clear focus and he could only say, "Woe to me!…I am ruined! For I am a man of unclean lips, and I live among a people of unclean lips" (Isaiah 6:5).

When we measure ourselves against other people, we may come out looking okay. In fact, measuring ourselves against other people might lead us to believe that we are fairly righteous in and of ourselves. But we cannot use other people as our moral measuring stick. *God* is the standard. And as we measure ourselves against God in His infinite holiness and righteousness, our sin shows up in all of its ugliness.

I remember Billy Graham telling a story that well illustrates how human sin shows up best in the light of God's holiness. Read his words:

> Several years ago I was to be interviewed at my home for a well-known television show and, knowing that it would appear on nationwide television, my wife took great pains to see that everything looked nice. She had vacuumed and dusted and tidied up the whole house and had gone over the living room with a fine-tooth comb since that was where the interview would be filmed.

> When the film crew arrived with all the lights and cameras, she felt that everything in that living room was spic and span. We were in place along with the interviewer when suddenly the television lights were turned on and we saw cobwebs

and dust where we had never seen them before. In the words of my wife: "That room was festooned with dust and cobwebs which simply did not show up under ordinary light."

The point is, of course, that no matter how well we clean up our lives and think we have them all in order, when we see ourselves in the light of God's Word, in the light of God's holiness, all the cobwebs and all the dust do show up.[1]

Jesus Explains the Depth of Human Sin

Jesus taught a great deal about human sin. In fact, He paints a rather bleak picture of the human predicament.

Jesus taught that since the Fall, all men and women are evil (Matthew 12:34) and are capable of great wickedness (Mark 7:20-23). Moreover, He said that man is utterly lost (Luke 19:10), that he is a sinner (Luke 15:10), that he is in need of repentance before a holy God (Mark 1:15), and that he needs to be born again (John 3:3,5,7).

Jesus often spoke of sin in metaphors that illustrate the havoc sin can wreak in a person's life. He described sin as blindness (Matthew 23:16-26), sickness (Matthew 9:12), being enslaved in bondage (John 8:34), and living in darkness (John 12:35-46). Moreover, Jesus taught that this is a universal condition and that all people are guilty before God (Romans 3:10-11).

Jesus also taught that both inner thoughts and external acts render a person guilty (Matthew 5:28). He taught that from within the human heart comes evil thoughts, sexual immorality, theft, murder, adultery, greed, malice, deceit, envy, slander, arrogance, and folly (Mark 7:21-23). He also affirmed that God is fully aware of every person's sins, both external acts and inner thoughts; nothing escapes His notice (John 4:17-19).

Because human sin is such a dire problem, a powerful cure or remedy is needed. What would you think of a doctor who, upon discovering that you had a huge tumor buried deep in your brain, responded, "Take two aspirin and you'll be just fine"? You'd think he was crazy!

In the same way, we must recognize that because man is so deeply engulfed in sin, a powerful remedy is called for. No spiritual Band-Aid will be sufficient for man's ailment. As we'll see in this book, that remedy is found in the person of Jesus Christ.

A Glimmer of Hope

Immediately after the Fall, God pronounced judgment against Adam, Eve, and Satan (the serpent). But as dark and depressing as this situation was, God also introduced a glimmer of hope into the scenario when He spoke to the serpent of the coming Redeemer: "I will put enmity between you and the woman, and between your offspring and hers; he will crush your head, and you will strike his heel" (Genesis 3:15).

The "offspring" of the woman is a reference to Jesus' future birth as a human being. His work on the cross would deal a fatal blow to Satan and his dark kingdom. Jesus would come as the Savior to bring salvation to all people who believe in Him. That is the good news of the gospel.

We'll talk more about this salvation throughout the rest of the book. We'll see that there is very good reason for saying that a personal relationship with Jesus—the Savior of humankind—is the very heart of Christianity.

⟶ *A Verse to Hide in Your Heart* ⟵

"The wages of sin is death, but the gift of God is eternal life in Christ Jesus our Lord."

ROMANS 6:23

Whereas sin caused estrangement between
man and God, Jesus at the cross brought
reconciliation and restoration.

SIX

From Corruption to New Creation: God's Solution

When man sinned, here's the problem God faced: How could God remain holy and just and at the same time forgive the sinner and allow the sinner into His presence? God's ineffable purity cannot tolerate sin. He is of purer eyes than to behold evil. How, then, could God deal justly with the sinner and at the same time exercise His compassion and save man from doom?

Whereas God's *justice* burned in wrath against man for outraging His holiness, God's *love* equally yearned to find a way to forgive him and bring him back into fellowship with Himself. But how could God express His love, His righteousness, and His justice toward man *all at the same time*?

God settled this problem in eternity past. Even before the creation of the world, God decreed the solution. He decreed a plan of salvation.

The Eternal Plan of Salvation

God is all-knowing. And because He is all-knowing, He knows the future just as clearly as He knows the past. What this means is that before man was even created, God already knew that man would fall into sin in the Garden of Eden. And because God knew that would happen, He came up with a plan of salvation before He even created man. *What an awesome God we have!*

Before the world began—indeed, in eternity past—God had already settled the issue of how He would bring about salvation for people. Scripture tells us that even before God created the world, He had decided that Jesus—as the "Lamb of God"—would die on the cross for the sins of man (Revelation 13:8). That was determined long, long ago.

This eternal plan of salvation would be carried out on earth, an insignificant planet when compared to the whole of God's magnificent universe. Although earth is a mere atom in comparison with the colossal stars of universal space, it is—in terms of God's redemptive plan—the center of the universe. *On earth* the Most High God entered into covenants with human beings in Old Testament times; *on earth* the Son of God became a man; and *on earth* stood the cross of the Redeemer.

Because the plan of salvation was formulated in eternity past and is being worked out in human history, we must come to regard human history from the standpoint of eternity. We must recognize a uniform plan, guided by God, which in the course of human history has been unfolding and will one day find its culmination when Christ comes again (at what is called the "second coming").

Human history in all its details, even the most minute, is but the outworking of the eternal purposes of God. Consider the words of theologian Robert Lightner:

> When viewed from the perspective of Scripture, history is more than the recording of the events

of the past. Rather, what has happened in the past, what is happening now, and what will happen in the future is all evidence of the unfolding of the purposeful plan devised by the personal God of the Bible. All the circumstances of life—past, present, and future—fit into the sovereign plan like pieces of a puzzle.[1]

What is fascinating to observe is that each of the three persons of the Trinity plays a significant role in the outworking of man's salvation.

The Father's Role

A careful reading of Scripture reveals that it was the Father's role to devise the plan of salvation (Ephesians 1:4). He sovereignly decreed it in eternity past (Romans 8:29-30). The Father works in an orderly way and has not left the salvation of humankind to haphazard and uncertain experimentation. He has a definite plan of salvation. This plan includes the means by which salvation is to be provided (Jesus' death on the cross), the objective that is to be realized (the forgiveness of sins), and the people who are to benefit (those who believe in Jesus).

Jesus' Role

God's glorious plan of salvation was conceived in eternity, but would be carried out by God in time. That which was eternally determined *before* the ages would be brought to fruition *in* the ages.

We learn from Scripture that this eternal plan was colossal in scope. According to the plan, the Father chose the Son (Jesus Christ) to be the Redeemer (1 Peter 1:18-21), and determined—among other things—to send Him into the world of humanity.

This is what Jesus was referring to when He told Nicodemus, "God did not send his Son into the world to condemn the world, but to save the world through him"

(John 3:17). On another occasion, Jesus told a large gathering of people, "I have come down from heaven not to do my will but to do the will of him who sent me" (John 6:38).

Jesus' task in the eternal plan of salvation included coming to earth as God's ultimate revelation (Hebrews 1:1-2), dying on the cross as a sacrifice for the sins of man (John 3:16), rising again from the dead (1 Peter 3:21), and being the Mediator (or "go-between") between the Father and humankind (1 Timothy 2:5). We were purchased with the precious blood of Christ, who was a lamb without blemish or defect.

Closely related to Christ's role in the eternal plan of salvation were the words uttered from His lips as He died upon the cross: "It is finished" (John 19:30). This proclamation is fraught with meaning. Surely the Lord was doing more than announcing the end of His physical life. That fact was self-evident. What was not known by the people who were crucifying Christ at Calvary was that somehow, despite the sin they were committing, God through Christ had completed the final sacrifice for sin.

The words "it is finished" are better translated from the Greek as "it *stands* finished." It seems clear that upon the cross the Son of God was announcing that the Father's eternal plan of salvation had been enacted in time and space. And the sacrificial aspect of that plan was now completed. Finally, the purpose for which Christ had come to earth came to fruition.

The Holy Spirit's Role

The Holy Spirit also has an important role in the outworking of the plan of salvation. Here are just a few of the notable ministries of the Holy Spirit:

- The Holy Spirit undertook the ministry of inspiring Scripture (2 Peter 1:21). He superintended the human authors of Scripture so that they wrote exactly what God wanted written.

This way we could learn all about God's plan of salvation.

- The Holy Spirit "regenerates" (or gives new life—*spiritual* life) to believers (Titus 3:5). The moment you believe in Jesus, the Holy Spirit gives you this new life.

- The Holy Spirit seals believers for the day of redemption (Ephesians 4:30). This means that believers are secure in their salvation. A "seal" indicates possession and security. God "possesses" believers as His children and He will see them securely into heaven.

- The Holy Spirit enables believers to overcome sin and gives them the power to live righteously (Galatians 5:22-23).

These and many other ministries show that the Holy Spirit plays a significant role in the plan of salvation. (We'll talk more about the Holy Spirit later in this book.)

Christ Our Redeemer

In Old Testament times, the phrase "kinsman-redeemer" was always used of a person who was related by blood to someone he was seeking to redeem from bondage or jail. If someone was sold into slavery, for example, it was the duty of a blood relative—the next of kin—to act as that person's kinsman-redeemer and buy him out of slavery (Leviticus 25:47-48).

Jesus is the Kinsman-Redeemer for sin-enslaved humanity. For Jesus to become a kinsman-redeemer, however, He had to become related by blood to the human race.

This indicates the necessity of the incarnation (a word that literally means "in the flesh"). Jesus *became a man*—He took on human "flesh" (without giving up His deity)—in order to redeem man (Hebrews 2:14-16). And because

Jesus was also fully God, His sacrificial death had infinite value (Hebrews 9:11-28).

The word *redemption* refers to "freedom by the payment of a price." The purchase price for our redemption from sin was the blood of Jesus. Because of what Christ accomplished at the cross, the believer is no longer a slave to sin and Satan.

Christ Our Savior

Related to Christ's role as Redeemer is His role as Savior. All throughout Old Testament times the prophets of God spoke of the coming of the Savior. This doctrine is at the very heart of God's eternal plan of salvation. From age to age the people of God had awaited and anticipated the birth of the Savior. And what an awesome moment it must have been when the Savior was finally born on earth in Bethlehem!

The Bible says that Jesus our Savior "gave himself as a ransom for all men" (1 Timothy 2:6). The word "ransom" refers to something given in exchange for another as the price of redemption. The idea is that of *substitution*—of Christ taking our place. Christ died to satisfy the demands of the offended righteousness of God. The Savior died in the sinner's place. He died as the sinner's substitute (Matthew 20:28). By so doing, He provided a salvation that people had absolutely no hope of obtaining for themselves.

Jesus affirmed that it was for the very purpose of dying that He came into the world (John 12:27). Moreover, He said His death was a sacrificial offering for the sins of humanity. (He said His blood "is poured out for many for the forgiveness of sins"—Matthew 26:26-28.) Jesus took His mission with utmost seriousness, for He knew that without Him, humanity would certainly perish (Matthew 16:25) and spend eternity apart from God in a place of great suffering (Luke 16:22-28).

Jesus therefore described His mission in the following ways: "The Son of Man did not come to be served, but to serve, and to give his life as a ransom for many" (Matthew 20:28).

"The Son of Man came to seek and to save what was lost" (Luke 19:10).

In John 10, Jesus compared Himself to a good shepherd who not only gives His life to save the sheep (John 10:11), but also lays His life down of His own accord (verse 18). That is precisely what Jesus did at the cross—He laid His life down as a sacrificial offering for the sins of humanity.

Certainly this is how other people perceived His mission. When Jesus began His three-year ministry and was walking toward John the Baptist at the Jordan River, John said, "Look, the Lamb of God, who takes away the sin of the world!" (John 1:29). John's portrayal of Christ as the Lamb of God is a graphic affirmation that Jesus Himself would be the sacrifice that would atone for the sins of humanity.

Christ was our substitute. He took our place. He took our sin upon Himself and provided salvation for us. *What an incredible exchange!*

I read about a small boy who was consistently late when he came home from school. One day his parents warned him that he must be home on time that afternoon. Instead, he arrived later than ever.

His mother met him at the door and said nothing. His father met him in the living room and said nothing.

At dinner that night, the boy looked at his plate. There was a small slice of bread and a cup of water. He looked at his father's full plate and then at his father, but his father remained silent. The boy was crushed.

The father waited for the full impact to sink in. Then, quietly, he took the boy's plate and placed it in front of himself. Next he took his own plate—full of meat and potatoes—and put it in front of the boy. Then he smiled at his son.

Years later, after that boy grew up, he said, "All my life I've known what God is like by what my father did that night."[2] What a great illustration this is of what Christ did for us—He took what was *ours* (sin) and gave us what was *His* (salvation, and a restored relationship with God).

Restored Fellowship

Though our sin put up a moral barrier between us and God so that fellowship was broken, through Jesus Christ that fellowship can be restored. One of my favorite devotional writers, A.W. Tozer, explains it this way:

> The whole work of God in redemption is to undo the tragic effects of that foul revolt, and to bring us back again into right and eternal relationship with Himself. This required that our sins be disposed of satisfactorily, that a full reconciliation be effected, and the way opened for us to return again into conscious communion with God and to live again in His Presence as before.[3]

Whereas sin caused separation, Jesus at the cross brought reconciliation. Whereas sin bred enmity between us and God, Jesus at the cross brought peace. Whereas sin created a gulf between man and God, Jesus at the cross bridged that gulf. Whereas sin broke the fellowship between us and God, Jesus at the cross restored it.

Again, then, we can only conclude that a personal relationship with Jesus is the very heart of Christianity. *And how blessed is that relationship!*

⌁ *A Verse to Hide in Your Heart* ⌁

"God so loved the world that he gave his one and only Son, that whoever believes in him shall not perish but have eternal life. For God did not send his Son into the world to condemn the world, but to save the world through him."

JOHN 3:16-17

Jesus' words and works demonstrate that He
is God. A personal relationship with Him is
the very heart of Christianity.

SEVEN

The Words and Works of Jesus Christ

Jesus asked one of His disciples, "Who do you say I am?" This is one of the most important questions in all history. *Who is Jesus Christ?* Christianity stands or falls on the identity and work of Jesus Christ.

Perhaps one of the best ways to understand the identity of Jesus Christ is to examine His own self-conception—that is, who He conceived of Himself to be. As we examine what the Scriptures say about this, it quickly becomes clear that Jesus was no ordinary man. Indeed, He understood Himself to be God.

Jesus' Self-Conception

Jesus' divine self-conception is revealed in at least three ways in the New Testament: 1) in the divine titles He used of Himself; 2) in His behavior; and 3) in the responses of people who were aware of His self-conception.

Revealed in His Titles

Jesus used many divine titles of Himself in the New Testament—including *Yahweh* (which is one of God's Old Testament names [John 8:58; Exodus 3:14]), *Lord* (Matthew 12:8), and *Son of God* (John 3:16-17). For illustration purposes, let's briefly examine the title Son of God as used in reference to Jesus Christ.

Perhaps no name or title of Christ has been so misunderstood. Some people have taken *Son of God* to mean that Christ came into existence at a point in time and that He is somehow inferior to the Father. Some people believe that since Christ is the Son of God, He cannot possibly be God in the same sense as the Father.

Such an understanding of the phrase is based on a faulty conception of what "Son of…" meant among the ancients. In biblical times the phrase "Son of…" was used to indicate *sameness of nature* and *equality of being.* So when Jesus claimed to be the Son of God, His Jewish contemporaries fully understood that He was making a claim to be God in an unqualified sense. Indeed, the Jews insisted, "We have a law, and according to that law he [Christ] must die, because he claimed to be the Son of God" (John 19:7). These Jews recognized that Jesus was identifying Himself as God, and they wanted to kill Him for committing blasphemy.

Scripture tells us that Christ's sonship is an eternal sonship. It is one thing to say that Jesus Christ *became* the Son of God; it is another thing altogether to say that He was *always* the Son of God. We must recognize that if there was a time when the Son was not the Son, then—to be consistent—there was also a time when the Father was not the Father.

One clear evidence of Christ's eternal sonship is that He is represented as *already being* the Son of God before His birth in Bethlehem. For example, recall Jesus' discussion with Nicodemus in John's Gospel. Jesus said, "God so loved the world that he *gave* his one and only Son, that whoever believes in him shall not perish but have eternal life. For God did not *send* his Son *into* the world to condemn the world, but to save the world through him" (John 3:16-17, emphasis added). That Christ—*as* the Son of God—was *sent* into the world implies that He was the Son of God *before* He took on human flesh.

Further evidence for Christ's eternal sonship is found in Hebrews 1:2, which says that God created the universe *through* His Son. Clearly, then, Christ was the Son of God prior to the creation. Moreover, Christ *as the Son* is explicitly said to have existed "before all things" (Colossians 1:13-17). As well, Jesus, speaking *as* the Son of God, asserts His eternal preexistence before Abraham (John 8:54-58).

When Jesus referred to Himself as the Son of God, He was pointing to His true identity as God, the second person of the eternal Trinity.

Revealed in His Behavior

Jesus' self-conception was often revealed in His behavior. His actions, as recorded in the Gospels, reveal that He believed Himself to be God.

Perhaps one of the clearest illustrations of this is found in Mark 2, where a paralytic—in hopes of a healing—was lowered through a roof by his friends so that he could get close to Jesus. Jesus' first words to the paralytic were, "Son, your sins are forgiven" (Mark 2:5).

Upon first reading, these words may seem out of place. Upon further reflection, however, it becomes obvious that Jesus was making an important statement. Jesus knew that all the people who were present were aware that only God could pronounce a person's sins as being forgiven. When Jesus said, "Your sins are forgiven," He was clearly placing Himself in the position of being God.

The scribes who were present understood Jesus' words this way, for they thought to themselves, "Why does this fellow talk like that? He's blaspheming! Who can forgive sins but God alone?" (Mark 2:7). Of course, Jesus' subsequent healing of the paralytic served to substantiate His claim to be God.

Jesus' self-conception was also evident in His portrayal of Himself as being the Judge of humankind. For example, at the end of the Sermon on the Mount, Jesus said that many people would one day come to Him saying, "Lord, Lord, did we not prophesy in Your name?" (Matthew 7:22). Jesus will tell these people that He never even knew them, and He will judge them accordingly.[1] This portrayal of Himself as the Judge of all humankind indicates that He believed Himself to be God.

Revealed in People's Responses

Jesus' self-conception was also revealed in the responses of various people who were aware of His self-conception. Throughout the Gospels, Jesus often received one of two responses that are polar opposites of each other: 1) people attempted to kill Him based on their belief that He had committed blasphemy, or 2) people worshiped Him.

An example of the first response is found in John 10:30, where Jesus told a group of Jewish critics, "I and the Father are one." His listeners immediately picked up rocks to stone Him to death. After all, the law prescribed the death penalty for anyone committing blasphemy.

In contrast, other people turned to Jesus in worship and praise. For example, in Matthew 14:33 Jesus is seen to accept worship from His disciples while afloat on the Sea of Galilee. Earlier, in Mark 14:3-9, Jesus is seen to accept worship from a woman who anointed Him with costly perfume. It is noteworthy that Jesus always accepted such worship as perfectly appropriate (Matthew 28:9; John 9:38). This in itself is an acclamation of deity.

Whether people picked up rocks to stone Jesus or they adored and worshiped Him, it is clear that both responses were simply a reflection of Jesus' self-conception that He was God.

Jesus' Words

Jesus' teachings were always presented as being ultimate and final. He never wavered in this. Jesus unflinchingly placed His teachings above those of Moses and the prophets. For Him to do that in a Jewish culture was both shocking and astonishing; the Jews saw Moses and the prophets as God's direct spokesmen, and for Jesus to go above them was to place Himself on par with God.

Jesus always spoke in His own authority. He never said, "Thus saith the Lord..." as did the prophets; He always said, "Verily, verily, I *say* unto you...." He never retracted anything He said, never guessed or spoke with uncertainty, never made revisions, never contradicted Himself, and never apologized for what He said. He even asserted that "heaven and earth will pass away, but my words will never pass away" (Mark 13:31), hence elevating His words directly to the realm of heaven.

Jesus' teachings had a profound effect on people. His listeners frequently recognized that His words were not the words of an ordinary man. When Jesus taught in Capernaum on the Sabbath, the people "were amazed at his teaching, because his message had authority" (Luke 4:32). After Jesus taught the Sermon on the Mount, "the crowds were amazed at his teaching, because he taught as one who had authority, and not as their teachers of the law" (Matthew 7:28-29). When some Jewish leaders asked the temple guards why they hadn't arrested Jesus when He spoke, they responded, "No one ever spoke the way this man does" (John 7:46).

We cannot read the Gospels long before recognizing that Jesus regarded Himself and His message as inseparable. The reason Jesus' teachings had ultimate authority was because He was (and is) God. The words of Jesus were the very words of God! Indeed, what mere *human* teacher would dare speak words like these to his peers?:

- "If anyone is thirsty, let him come to me and drink. Whoever believes in me, as the Scripture has said, streams of living water will flow from within him" (John 7:37-38).

- "Peace I leave with you; my peace I give to you. I do not give to you as the world gives" (John 14:27).

- "I am the bread of life. He who comes to me will never go hungry, and he who believes in me will never be thirsty" (John 6:35).

- "Come to me, all you who are weary and burdened, and I will give you rest" (Matthew 11:28).

- "I have come that they may have life, and have it to the full" (John 10:10).

To give His words the stamp of divine authority, Jesus often performed a miracle immediately following a teaching. For example, after telling the paralytic that his sins were forgiven, Jesus healed him to prove He had the divine authority to forgive sins (Mark 2:1-12). After telling Martha that He was "the resurrection and the life," He raised her brother Lazarus from the dead—thereby proving the veracity and authority of His words (John 11:17-44). After rebuking His disciples for having too little faith, Jesus calmed a raging storm to show they had good reason to place their faith in Him (Matthew 8:23-27).

Jesus' Works

John's Gospel always refers to Jesus' miracles as "signs." This word emphasizes the *significance* of the action rather than the marvel (John 4:54; 6:14; 9:16). These signs were strategically performed by Jesus to signify His true identity and glory.

When John the Baptist was in prison, he sent his disciples to ask Jesus, "Are you the one who was to come, or should we expect someone else?" (Matthew 11:3). Jesus replied to them, "Go back and report to John what you hear and see: The blind receive sight, the lame walk, those who have leprosy are cured, the deaf hear, the dead are raised, and the good news is preached to the poor" (Matthew 11:4-5). By saying this, Jesus was reminding John that these signs were precisely what was predicted of the Messiah (Isaiah 29:18-21; 35:5-6; 61:1).

John's Gospel tells us that Jesus' signs were performed in the presence of His disciples to ensure that there was adequate witness to the events that transpired (John 20:30). *Witness* is a pivotal concept in this Gospel; the word occurs some 47 times and the reason for this is clear. *The signs performed by Jesus are thoroughly attested.* There were many witnesses. Therefore, the signs cannot be dismissed or explained away!

These signs were presented "that you may believe that Jesus is the Christ, the Son of God" (John 20:31). The signs in John's Gospel, then, give indisputable evidence that Jesus is the Christ and the Son of God.

It is not our goal here to examine every miracle or sign performed by Jesus. But we will look at three kinds of signs that clearly attest to His identity. These are miracles no mere human could accomplish.

1. Jesus Controlled the Realm of Nature. Over and over again in the Gospels, Jesus displayed a power over natural forces that could belong only to God, the author of these forces. This should not surprise us, for Christ Himself is the Creator (Colossians 1:16). We should fully expect Christ to exercise control over that which He brought into being.

This is illustrated for us at a wedding banquet in Galilee, where Jesus had some servants fill six stone water jars—each holding 20 to 30 gallons—and turned the water (over 120 gallons) into wine (John 2:1-11). "This, the first of his miraculous signs, Jesus performed in Cana of Galilee. He thus revealed his glory, and his disciples put their faith in him" (verse 11).

Shortly thereafter, Jesus multiplied five small loaves of bread and two small fish into enough food to satisfy over 5,000 people—and there were 12 baskets of leftovers (John 6:1-15)! That evening, Jesus walked on the surface of a lake out to His disciples' boat, which was a considerable distance from land (6:16-21). After witnessing this miracle, the disciples worshiped Jesus in the boat, saying, "Truly you are the Son of God" (*see* Matthew 14:33). Turning water into wine, multiplying food, walking on water—these are not feats mere mortals can do!

2. Jesus Healed People of Bodily Afflictions. Just as Jesus the Creator could sovereignly control the realm of nature, so also could He heal human bodies. Jesus' ministry of healing sick people is a direct fulfillment of messianic prophecies in the Old Testament. One of these, Isaiah 35:5-6, predicted that when the Messiah came, "then will the eyes of the blind be opened and the ears of the deaf unstopped. Then will the lame leap like a deer, and the mute tongue shout for joy."

On one occasion, a royal official came to Jesus and informed Him that his son was sick in Capernaum. He begged Jesus to come and heal the lad—who, at the time, was near death. Jesus immediately granted the request and uttered a single, authoritative pronouncement: "You may go. Your son will live" (John 4:50). The official would soon discover that his son was healed at the precise time Jesus had granted his request (verses 51-53)! Jesus likewise healed an invalid (5:1-15), a blind man (9:1-12), and many other people—thereby proving beyond all doubt that He was the long-awaited Messiah.

3. Jesus Raised People from the Dead. Based on their understanding of the Old Testament Scriptures, the Jews believed that God is the only source of life. At the Creation, "the LORD God formed the man from the dust of the ground and breathed into his nostrils the breath of life, and the man became a living being" (Genesis 2:7). First Samuel 2:6 affirms that "the LORD brings death and makes alive; he brings down to the grave and raises up." This is why Jesus sent shock waves through the first-century Jewish community when He raised people from the dead.

Jesus' power to restore life is vividly illustrated in John chapter 11. Jesus had been informed that His friend Lazarus was seriously ill, but He told the disciples that "this sickness will not end in death. No, it is for God's glory so that God's Son may be glorified through it" (John 11:4). Later, after *purposefully* delaying His visit to Lazarus, He omnisciently informed the disciples that Lazarus had died.

As promised, however, Jesus was glorified in what transpired. For at His command, Lazarus was raised from the dead—thereby attesting to the truthfulness of His words to Martha, who was Lazarus's sister: "I am the resurrection and the life. He who believes in me will live, even though he dies; and whoever lives and believes in me will never die" (John 11:25-26).

John's Gospel tells us that "Jesus did many other miraculous signs in the presence of his disciples, which are not recorded in this book. But these are written that you may believe that Jesus is the Christ, the Son of God, and that by believing you may have life in his name" (John 20:30). In each miracle Jesus performed—whether it involved controlling the realm of nature, healing people of physical afflictions, or raising people from the dead—He distinguished Himself from weak and mortal man and attested to His true identity as Messiah-God.

As marvelous as Jesus' miracles were, none of them compare with His greatest miracle of all—His resurrection from the dead. Let us briefly examine the Scriptures on Jesus' death and resurrection.

Jesus' Death on the Cross

After Jesus died on the cross, His body was buried in accordance with Jewish burial customs. He was wrapped in a linen cloth, and about 100 pounds of aromatic spices—mixed together to form a gummy substance—were applied to the wrappings of cloth around His body.

After His body was placed in a solid rock tomb, an extremely large stone was rolled by means of levers against the entrance. This stone would have weighed up to four tons (8,000 pounds). It is not a stone that would have been easily moved by human beings.

Roman guards were then stationed at the tomb. These strictly disciplined men were highly motivated in their duties. Fear of cruel punishment by the Roman government produced flawless attention to duty, especially in the night watches. These Roman guards would have affixed the Roman seal on the tomb, a stamp representing Rome's sovereign power and authority.

All this makes the situation at the tomb following Christ's resurrection highly significant. The Roman seal had been broken, an offense that carried an automatic penalty of crucifixion upside down for the person who did it. Moreover, the large stone was moved a substantial distance from the entrance, as if it had been picked up like a pebble and plucked out of the way. The Roman guards had also fled. Since the penalty for a guard leaving his position was death, we can assume they must have had a substantial reason for fleeing!

We learn the details of what happened in Matthew 28:1-6:

After the Sabbath, at dawn on the first day of the week, Mary Magdalene and the other Mary went to look at the tomb. There was a violent earth-quake, for an angel of the Lord came down from heaven and, going to the tomb, rolled back the stone and sat on it.

His appearance was like lightning, and his clothes were white as snow. The guards were so afraid of him that they shook and became like dead men. The angel said to the women, "Do not be afraid, for I know that you are looking for Jesus, who was crucified. He is not here; he has risen, just as he said."

The rest is history. The women were filled with joy and ran to tell the disciples the glorious news. *Christ is risen!*

The Evidence for Christ's Resurrection

Jesus Christ rose bodily from the dead. The biblical evidence for this is abundant: The tomb was empty (Luke 24:3). The risen Jesus showed His disciples both "his hands and side" (John 20:20). He ate three different times (Luke 24:41-43; John 21:5-14; Acts 1:4; 10:41). He appeared bodily to more than 500 people at the same time (1 Corinthians 15:6). And He made numerous other appearances.

Of course, there have been many attempts in recent years to explain away the resurrection of Christ. One of the most popular of these is that Jesus' followers "made up" the resurrection story.

However, it's hard to believe that Jesus' followers—predominantly Jewish and therefore aware of God's stern commandments against lying and bearing false witness—would make up such a lie, and then suffer and *give up their own lives in defense of it*. Moreover, if Jesus' followers concocted events like the resurrection, wouldn't Jesus' critics have then immediately come forward to debunk these lies and put an end to Christianity once and for all? *Yet His critics were silent*—for the evidence for Christ's resurrection was overwhelming and undeniable.

Jesus Just a Good Moral Teacher?

Some people today have claimed that Jesus was just a great example or a moral teacher for us. Such an idea is preposterous. No mere "example" or "moral teacher" would ever claim that the destiny of the world lay in His hands, or that people would spend eternity in heaven or hell depending on whether they believed in Him (John 6:26-40). The only "example" this would provide would be one of lunacy.

And for Jesus to convince people that He was God (John 8:58) and the Savior of the world (Luke 19:10)—when He really wasn't—would be the ultimate *immorality*. There's no way to feasibly argue that Jesus was *just* a good moral teacher.

Jesus One of Many Ways to God?

Still other people have claimed that Jesus is just "one of many ways to God." This line of thinking tries to argue that all the leaders of all the world religions were pointing to the same God.

The folly of this idea becomes quickly evident by contrasting the doctrine of God (the most fundamental of all doctrines) in the various religions. For example:

- Jesus taught that there is only one personal God who is triune in nature (Matthew 28:19).

- Muhammad taught that there is only one God, but that God cannot have a son.

- Confucius believed in many gods.

- Zoroaster taught that there is both a good god and a bad god.

- Buddha taught that the concept of God was essentially irrelevant. Obviously, these religious leaders were not pointing to the same God. If one is right, all the others are wrong.

Jesus claimed that what He said took precedence over all others. He said He is humanity's only means of coming into a relationship with God. He affirmed, "I am the way and the truth and the life. No one comes to the Father except through me" (John 14:6). In Acts 4:12 Peter affirmed, "Salvation is found in no one else, for there is no other name under heaven given to men by which we must be saved."

Moreover, Christianity is a religion *of history*. The apostle Paul warned the religious men of Athens of an impending objective event: the divine judgment of all humanity. And he based this warning on the objective, historical evidence for the resurrection of Jesus (Acts 17:31).

It was this historical resurrection that instilled such boldness in the disciples. Initially, when Jesus was arrested, "all the disciples deserted him and fled" (Matthew 26:56). But after Jesus' resurrection, these fearful cowards became steel bulwarks of the faith. They remained unflinching in their commitment to Christ, even in the face of great personal danger and death.

Jesus, the Fulfillment of Prophecy

One evidence that proves that Jesus is the divine Messiah is that He is the fulfillment of virtually hundreds of messianic prophecies in the Old Testament. This includes prophecies Jesus couldn't possibly have conspired to fulfill, such as His birthplace (Micah 5:2), being born of a virgin (Isaiah 7:14), and the identity of His forerunner, John the Baptist (Malachi 3:1).

Mathematically speaking, there is something like a 1 in 10^{17} (or 1 in 100,000,000,000,000,000) chance of one man fulfilling just eight of the hundreds of messianic prophecies in the Old Testament. Peter Stoner, the author of *Science Speaks*, provides an illustration to help us understand the magnitude of such odds:

> Suppose that we take 10^{17} silver dollars and lay them on the face of Texas. They will cover all of the state two feet deep. Now mark one of these silver dollars and stir the whole mass thoroughly, all over the state. Blindfold a man and tell him that he can travel as far as he wishes, but he must pick up one silver dollar and say that this is the right one. What chance would he have of getting the right one? Just the same chance that the prophets would have had of writing these eight prophecies and having them all come true in any one man, from their day to the present time, providing they wrote using their own wisdom.[2]

Jesus fulfilled not just eight but hundreds of messianic prophecies in the Old Testament. *Truly He is the promised Messiah!*

A Personal Relationship with Jesus

Jesus often spoke of the need to have a personal relationship with Him. Jesus once said, "Come to me, all you who are weary and burdened, and I will give you rest" (Matthew 11:28). This verse does not say "come to the church" or "come to a Bible study" to obtain rest. Certainly going to church and Bible studies are important. But *Jesus is the center of Christianity.* We are to go to Him, and in our relationship with Him we will find spiritual rest for our souls.

Jesus told some Jewish people, "You diligently study the Scriptures because you think that by them you possess eternal life. These are the Scriptures that testify about me, yet you refuse to come to me to have life" (John 5:39-40). Again, we find that Christianity is not just the Bible or knowledge about the doctrines of the Bible. We go to the Bible to meet Jesus. A relationship with Jesus is the heart of Christianity.

We do not go to the Scriptures as an end in themselves. Rather than seeking eternal life in the Scriptures, we seek eternal life in Jesus Christ, whom the Scriptures speak about.

Christ is the theme that binds the whole Bible together. The Old Testament law lays a foundation for the coming of Christ. The prophets speak of the expectation of Christ. The gospels speak of the manifestation of Christ. And the epistles address the interpretation of Christ.

Just as Jesus is the very heart of the Bible, so also is Jesus the heart of Christianity.

~~ *A Verse to Hide in Your Heart* ~~

"Jesus answered, 'I am the way and the truth and the life. No one comes to the Father except through me.'"

JOHN 14:6

Jesus Christ
The Heart of the Bible

Jesus affirmed that the Scriptures were "concerning himself" (Luke 24:27), were "written about me" (verse 44), were "written of me" (Hebrews 10:7 NASB), and "bear witness to me" (John 5:39 NASB).

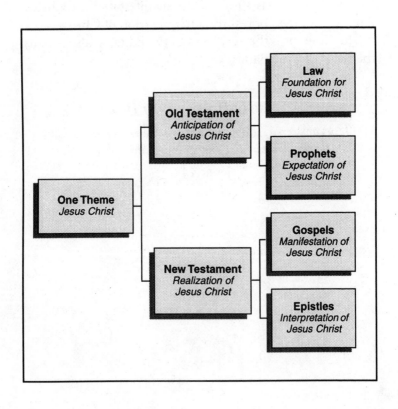

┌─────── ...The Heart of the Matter ───────┐

Salvation is a free gift from God and is
received by placing faith in Jesus Christ.

└──┘

EIGHT

How to Receive the Gift of Salvation

A personal relationship with Jesus is the single most important relationship you can have. To have a relationship with Him is to have a relationship with God Almighty. But how does a person enter into this relationship?

God has not made the gospel complicated. In fact, according to the New Testament, a relationship with Jesus begins simply by placing faith in Him. This may sound too good to be true, yet it is the clear teaching of Scripture. Some people try to add certain good works as a condition for salvation, but this goes against Scripture. The Bible portrays salvation as a free gift that we receive by faith alone.

A key verse you will want to make note of is Acts 16:31. In this verse we find the apostle Paul and his companion Silas in jail. The jailer asked Paul and Silas how he could become saved. They responded quite forthrightly, "Believe in the Lord Jesus, and you will be saved" (Acts

16:31). The jailer then believed and became saved *at that moment.*

One moment the jailer was not saved. The next moment he was. And the factor that brought him salvation was exercising simple faith in Jesus.

Close to 200 times in the New Testament, salvation is said to be *by faith alone*—with no works in sight. Consider the following:

- In John 5:24 Jesus says, "I tell you the truth, whoever hears my word and believes him who sent me has eternal life and will not be condemned; he has crossed over from death to life."

- In John 11:25 Jesus says, "I am the resurrection and the life. He who believes in me will live, even though he dies."

- In John 12:46 Jesus says, "I have come into the world as a light, so that no one who believes in me should stay in darkness."

Clearly, salvation is by faith in Christ!

If salvation were not by faith alone, then Jesus' message in the Gospel of John—manifest in the above quotations— would be deceptive. That is, if salvation is obtained by both faith *and* good works, then it would have been deceptive of Jesus to say so many times that there is only one condition for salvation—faith.

Having said this, it is also true that according to Scripture we are saved *by* faith but *for* good works. That is, works are not the *condition* of our salvation, but are a *consequence* of it. We are saved not by works, but by the kind of faith that *ends up producing* works. (We'll talk more about this issue shortly.)

Now, there is nothing complicated about faith. Actually, faith is central to all of life. A good example would be the act of going to a doctor. We go to a doctor to be treated, and in many cases we are unfamiliar with the doctor's training and degree. Yet by faith we trust his diagnosis of our ailment. Then, by faith we go to a pharmacy and have a prescription filled and take a medicine with a strange name based on our belief that the doctor knows what he's doing. All this takes place by faith.

Placing faith in Jesus Christ involves taking Him at His word. Faith involves believing that Christ was who He said He was. It also involves believing that Christ can do what He claimed He could do—He can forgive me and come into my life. Faith is an act of commitment in which I open the door of my heart to Him.

When I was younger, I thought I was a Christian simply because I attended church and, in general, did more good things than bad things. I figured that as long as my good deeds outweighed my bad deeds by the time I died, I would be saved. But nothing could be further from the truth. As I noted earlier in this book, going to church doesn't make a person a Christian any more than standing in a garage makes a person an automobile.

It was only when I came to understand that salvation is received by faith in Christ that I became a Christian at age 18. And what a wondrous day that was. No longer did I try to *earn* salvation. I became saved by simply believing in Jesus.

Some years after I became a Christian, I was ministering at a Christian coffeehouse called Mainstream in downtown Houston, Texas. I figured it would just be a routine night. But while I was there, a member of the Hell's Angels motorcycle gang walked in. He was wearing lots of black leather. He walked over to me and started talking.

He said that the previous night he and his brother, who was also a Hell's Angel member, had been in a gang fight. His brother had been fatally stabbed. And just before he died, he told his surviving brother, "Go to Mainstream."

I don't know how the dying brother knew about this coffeehouse. But by God's providence, a Hell's Angel visited us that night and within a half hour he placed saving faith in Jesus Christ and his life was changed forever.

The gospel is for all people. Anyone can be set free by believing in Jesus. Just as this Hell's Angel became a Christian by believing in Jesus, so also can anyone be saved by believing in Jesus.

Salvation Is a Gift of Grace

Grace is often hard for us to understand. After all, our society is performance-oriented. Good grades in school depend on how well we perform on our schoolwork. Climbing up the corporate ladder depends on how well we perform at our job. Nothing of real worth is a "free ticket" in our society. But God's gift of salvation is a grace-gift. The word *grace* means "undeserved favor." Because salvation is a grace-gift, it can't be earned. *It's free!* We can't attain it by a good performance.

Consider the following verses:

- Ephesians 2:8-9 says, "By grace you have been saved, through faith—and this not from yourselves, it is the gift of God—not by works, so that no one can boast."

- Titus 3:5 tells us that God "saved us, not on the basis of deeds which we have done in righteousness, but according to His mercy" (NASB).

- Romans 3:20 says that "by the works of the Law no flesh will be justified [or, declared righteous] in His sight" (NASB, insert added).

In Galatians 2:16 the apostle Paul tells us that "we may be justified by faith in Christ and not by observing the law." We must recognize that grace and meritorious works are mutually exclusive. Romans 11:6 says this about God's salvation: "If by grace, then is it no longer by works; if it were, grace would no longer be grace."

Gifts cannot be worked for—only wages can be worked for. As Romans 4:4-5 tells us, "When a man works, his wages are not credited to him as a gift, but as an obligation. However, to the man who does not work but trusts God who justifies the wicked, his faith is credited as righteousness." Since salvation is a free gift, it cannot be earned.

The person who seeks salvation through self-effort is like the man who, in attempting to sail across the Atlantic Ocean, found his sailboat becalmed for days with no wind. Finally, frustrated by his lack of progress, he tried to make his stalled sailboat move by pushing against the mast. Through strenuous effort, he succeeded in making the boat rock back and forth, and thereby created a few small waves on the otherwise smooth sea. Seeing the waves and feeling the rocking of the boat, he assumed he was making progress and so continued his efforts. However, though he exerted himself a great deal, he actually got nowhere.[1]

So it is with salvation. Our efforts to save ourselves are futile. It cannot be done. No matter how hard we try, it is no use. The source of salvation lies in God's grace, not in exertions of will-power, or in efforts of discipline, or any other self-effort. *Salvation is a free gift!*

What About Repentance?

To be sure, repentance is involved in becoming a child of God, but the term must be carefully defined. The word *repent* literally means "a change of mind toward something or someone." The word is not limited to contexts dealing with sin.

Repentance as it relates to Jesus Christ, for example, means to change our mind about Him—who He is and what He's done to provide forgiveness and deliverance from our sins. Repentance in this sense refers to changing our mind about the particular sin of rejecting Christ.

In the book of Acts the Jews had rejected Jesus as being the Messiah. So when they were admonished to repent and believe in Jesus (Acts 2:38; 3:19), they were actually being admonished to change their minds about Jesus—*who He was* and *what He had done*—and believe in Him as the Messiah/Savior so their sins could be forgiven.

People everywhere are called to do the same. Instead of rejecting Christ, we are to change our minds about Him and believe in Him as the Messiah/Savior.

Why Did God Give Us the Law?

A question that often comes up is, If salvation is a free gift received by faith in Christ, then why did God give us the law (or "commandments"—such as the Ten Commandments)? That's an important question—so much so that we must answer it at length.

There are a number of reasons why God gave us the law. As we have already seen, however, God did *not* give us the law as a means of attaining salvation. Remember, Romans 3:20 says that "no one will be declared righteous in his sight by observing the law."

So why did God give us the law? First, to show us what sin is. The law set up God's holy standards of conduct. The law also shows us the consequences if we don't measure up to those high standards. God did this purposefully, for as we grow to see that we don't measure up to the holy standards of the law, we're all forced to admit that we have a sin problem.

Second, though this may sound very strange to you, another purpose of the law is to provoke sin all the more in people. Scripture tells us that the law was given to us so that "trespass [or sin] might increase" (Romans 5:20). (It's somewhat like the child who immediately decides to do the very thing his mom just told him not to do. Mom's "law" provoked sin.) You see, God wants us to become so overwhelmed with the sin problem that we cannot deny its reality and severity. He wants us all to see how much we need the Savior, Jesus Christ. The law, by provoking sin to increase, effectively points us to the dire need for a Savior. And, as the apostle Paul said, "where sin increased, *grace increased all the more*" (verse 20, emphasis added).

Still another very important function of the law is that it is like a tutor that leads us to Christ (Galatians 3:24-25). Among the ancient Romans, it was the job of a tutor to lead a child to school. Likewise, the law is our tutor in leading us straight to Jesus Christ, the Savior. The law does this by showing us our sin and then pointing to the marvelous grace of Christ.

Once we have "arrived" to Christ—trusting in Him as our Savior—the law has done its job and it no longer holds sway over us. For believers "Christ is the end of the law so that there may be righteousness for everyone who believes" (Romans 10:4).

This brings to mind the story of a man who lived in a country where the laws stated that people could not walk outside on the sidewalks after 6:00 P.M. Eventually this man moved to the United States.

After arriving in the States he decided to see the sights and so went for a long walk. Suddenly he realized it was getting close to 6:00 P.M. and he was far from his hotel. In desperation, he stopped a stranger who was getting into a car and, and in halting English, said, "Please, sir, help me! It is almost six o'clock and I am too far from my hotel to walk back before I will be arrested. Can you give me a ride?"

The stranger at first was confused, but then realized that the man was new to the United States. So he said, "Sir, let me assure you that in the United States we do not arrest people for being out after six."

This man knew he was in a new country, but he had not cast off his obedience to the laws of his old country and so was still being controlled by what no longer had any jurisdiction over him. He was a free man, needlessly bound to the rules and regulations of his former life.[2]

Christians are sometimes the same way. They forget that for believers "Christ is the end of the law" (Romans 10:4). Because they forget that truth, they continue trying to earn favor with God by attempting to perfectly obey God's law—even after trusting in Christ for the forgiveness of all their sins.

You and I as Christians are to focus our attention on Christ and seek to walk in moment-by-moment dependence upon the Holy Spirit. As we do this, God Himself progressively brings our lives into conformity with the holiness that is reflected in the law. If we instead focus our primary concern on external obedience to God's law, then we're focusing on the *results* of the Christian life instead of on the *source* of it—Jesus Christ. This is a sure path to defeat.

The story has been told of a do-it-yourselfer who went into a hardware store early one morning and asked for a saw. The salesman took a chain saw from the shelf and commented that it was their "newest model, with the latest in technology, guaranteed to cut ten cords of firewood a day." The customer thought that sounded good, so he bought it on the spot.

The next day the customer returned, looking somewhat exhausted. "Something must be wrong with this saw," he moaned. "I worked as hard as I could and only managed to cut three cords of wood. I used to do four with my old-fashioned saw."

Looking confused, the salesman said, "Here, let me try it out back on some wood we keep here." They went to the woodpile, the salesman pulled the cord, and as the motor went *Vvvrooommm*, the customer leaped back and exclaimed, "What's that noise?"[3]

The customer who tried to saw wood without the power of the saw to help him is very much like the believer who attempts to live the Christian life without the daily empowerment of the Spirit. He is on the path to defeat. We are called to walk in dependence upon the Spirit, and the Spirit Himself works in our lives to bring about the righteousness reflected in the law. Only He can give us the power to walk in a way pleasing to God.

Remember—We Are Accepted "In Christ"

One way to prevent depending on our good works for our salvation is to remember that believers are "in Christ" (Ephesians 2:7). At the moment you trust in Christ for salvation, a wonderful thing happens. You are identified with Christ. You are joined in spiritual union to Him. Not only are your sins taken care of by Christ, but He also imputes His own righteousness to you. This means that when God the Father looks at you, He sees you through the lens or filter of His Son, who is perfectly holy and righteous.

Because of the wonderful grace of God, you are accepted by God not on the basis of your works but on the basis that you are in Christ. And because the Father accepts Christ perfectly, He also accepts you perfectly because you are in Christ.

Now, as might be expected, Satan seeks to blind our minds to this glorious and liberating truth. His goal is to keep us from focusing on our identity in Christ and focus instead on the need to do good works in order to earn favor with God.

Then, when we fail to live up to the standards of God's law, Satan shifts his attention to making us feel like a worm before God. He wants us to feel guilt and despondency over our consistent failure to meet God's demands.

This in turn leads to a sense of alienation and separation from God. If we think that God has something against us because of some sin we've committed, it's natural for us to back off and alienate ourselves from Him. That is what Adam and Eve did after they sinned—they tried to hide from God. The more we think God is angry at us, the more alienated and estranged we feel from Him. Satan loves to get us into this mode of thinking.

The fact is, though, that Christians who give in to this line of thinking have forgotten their state of grace before God. They have forgotten that they are in Christ and that the Father sees them as being in Christ. The moment they take their eyes off the reality that they are in Christ—and that the Father accepts them on that basis—they immediately try to start earning God's forgiveness through good works.

But, as I've pointed out earlier, we don't do good works to earn favor with God. Our favor with God comes as a result of placing faith in Christ, after which time the Father sees us as being in Christ. In our everyday living, we may still be quite imperfect. But the Father sees us as having the very perfection of Christ since we are in Christ. As a result of our relationship with Christ, and as a result of walking in dependence on the Spirit, good works will naturally be produced in our lives. Good works, then, are the result of our relationship with Christ, not the source of it.

One of my favorite passages in the Bible is Psalm 130:3-4: "If you, O LORD, kept a record of sins, O LORD, who could stand? But with you there is forgiveness." The phrase "kept a record" was an accounting term among the ancients. It refers to keeping an itemized account.

The point of that passage is that if we think God is keeping a detailed account of all our sins, there would be no way for us to have a relationship with Him. It would be impossible. The good news is that God does not keep such an account, but rather forgives those who trust in Christ.

What Should I Do When I Sin?

Even though our salvation is based totally on God's grace, it's important to understand that it's never okay for the Christian to "feel free to sin" after he's been saved. That most certainly is not the teaching of Scripture.

Once you become a part of the family of God, God begins to work a transformation in your life so that you reflect more and more the family likeness (that is, holiness). Of course, in this life we will never reach sinless perfection. But, as time passes, we will become increasingly aware of how God is working righteousness into our daily experience.

When we get to heaven, we will no longer have the sin nature in us. We will no longer sin at all. That's a day to look forward to! But until then, we need to deal with sin on a daily basis. Why? Because when we sin we break our fellowship with the Father. (Don't misunderstand. Only our *fellowship* is broken—not our *standing* as a member of God's family. That standing is secure.) When we break our fellowship with the Father through sin, we need to deal with sin so fellowship can be restored. Here's how it works:

When we (as Christians) sin, the Holy Spirit convicts us and we experience a genuine sense of conviction that Scripture calls a "godly sorrow" (2 Corinthians 7:8-11). If we fail to properly relate this sorrow to the forgiveness we have in Christ, it leads to a sense of guilt and a sense of estrangement from God. So, what do we do when the Holy Spirit convicts us of a sin?

Scripture says we need to confess that sin to God (1 John 1:9). The Greek word for confess literally means "to say the same thing." So, when we confess our sin to God, that means we're saying the same thing about our sin that God says about it. We're agreeing with God that we did wrong. No excuses! And following my confession, I can thank God that in His sight my sin is *already forgiven*, because Jesus paid for it on the cross. Instantly my fellowship with the Father is restored. Then, my goal from that point forward is to walk in the power of the Holy Spirit so I'll have the power to resist such sins in the future.

What happens if the Christian refuses to respond to the Holy Spirit's conviction and chooses to continue sinning? That is not a wise thing to do. God loves us too much to let us perpetually remain in sin. Scripture reveals that if a child of God sins and refuses to turn from it and confess it, God—with a motive of love—brings discipline into his or her life to bring him or her to a point of confession (Hebrews 12:4-11). God's desire is to restore fellowship with His child.

It's much the same in a human family. If my son or daughter does something wrong, and refuses to turn from it, I may find it necessary to discipline that child. Now, that child is still in my family. Nothing will change that. But because I love my child, I can't let him or her persist in doing wrong without taking action. In the same way, because God loves us, He takes disciplinary action when we refuse to turn from sin and confess it.

Should I Get Baptized?

There's one final issue we need to deal with in this chapter. Many sincere people have wondered whether baptism is a requirement for salvation.

I do not believe it is. Please don't misunderstand; there's no question that baptism is important, and it should be among the first acts of obedience to God following our conversion to Christ. But in itself, baptism is not a *requirement* for salvation.

There are several observations from Scripture that lead me to this conclusion. First, when Jesus was crucified, two thieves were crucified along with Him. One of them placed his faith in Christ while he was hanging on his cross. And Jesus immediately said to him, "I tell you the truth, today you will be with me in paradise" (Luke 23:43). The thief had no opportunity to jump down from the cross and get baptized, but he was still saved.

Second, in Acts 10 we find Cornelius—a devout Gentile—placing faith in Christ and becoming saved. Yet the account in Acts 10 makes it clear that Cornelius was saved prior to being baptized in water. At the moment Cornelius believed in Christ, the gift of the Holy Spirit was poured out on him (Acts 10:45). The fact that the Holy Spirit came upon Cornelius prior to being baptized shows that he was saved before his baptism.

And third, in 1 Corinthians 1:17 the apostle Paul said, "Christ did not send me to baptize, but to preach the gospel." Here a distinction is made between the gospel and being baptized. We are told elsewhere that it is the gospel that brings salvation (1 Corinthians 15:2). Because baptism is not a part of that gospel, it is not necessary for salvation. Nevertheless, we should still get baptized because God has instructed us to.

We must keep in mind the purpose of baptism. In the New Testament, baptism is portrayed as a symbol of our death and resurrection with Jesus Christ. Going down into the water symbolizes our death with Christ, and rising up out of the water symbolizes our resurrection and new life with Christ. So, baptism is symbolic, and it is a way of making public our identification with Jesus Christ.

In a way, baptism is like a wedding ring: they both symbolize transactions. A wedding ring symbolizes marriage; baptism symbolizes salvation in Jesus Christ. The mere wearing of a wedding ring does not make a person married any more than being baptized makes a person saved. But both the wedding ring and baptism symbolize marriage and a saved state.

My friend, have you received the free gift of salvation? Do you have a personal relationship with Jesus? If not, *why not start that relationship today?* "Now is the day of salvation" (2 Corinthians 6:2).

⟶ *A Verse to Hide in Your Heart* ⟵

*"By grace you have been saved, through faith;
and this not from yourselves, it is the gift of God—
not by works, so that no one can boast."*

EPHESIANS 2:8-9

> Our salvation in Christ involves unfathomable
> spiritual blessings.

NINE

The Blessings of Salvation

Suppose your best friend came by one day with a special gift for you. How would you respond? Would you immediately pull out your wallet to pay for the gift? Of course not. To do so would be a great insult.

A gift must be accepted for what it is—something freely given and unmerited. If you have to pay for a gift or do something to deserve or earn it, it is not really a gift. True gifts are freely given and freely received. To attempt to give or receive a gift in any other manner makes it not a gift.

It is the same way with our salvation in Jesus Christ. God offers us salvation as a free gift. He does not attach strings to it, because to do so would make it something other than a gift. Any attempt on our part (no matter how small) to pay for our salvation by doing something is an insult to God.

No one in heaven will ever be able to say, "Look at me! I made it! With a little help from God, I made it!" Salvation is all by God. Not even the smallest part of it is the result of anything we do or don't do.

As God says in His Word, "It is by grace you have been saved, through faith—and this not from yourselves, it is the gift of God—not by works, so that no one can boast" (Ephesians 2:8-9). Salvation is 100-percent accomplished by God.

Now, there are far more blessings that go along with our salvation in Christ than can be covered in a single chapter. But in the little that we cover here, I think you'll agree that the blessings of salvation are astounding.

We Are Born Again

Being born again literally means to be "born from above." It refers to God's act of giving eternal life to the person who believes in Christ (Titus 3:5).

Being born again places a person in God's eternal family (1 Peter 1:23). Just as a physical birth places a new baby into a family, so also does a spiritual birth place a person into the family of God.

In John 3 Jesus spoke with a man named Nicodemus and told him about the need to be born again. Nicodemus was a Pharisee (a Jewish leader) who would have been trusting in his physical descent from Abraham for entrance into heaven. The Jews believed that because they were physically related to Abraham, they were in a specially privileged position before God.

Jesus, however, denied such a possibility. The fact is, parents can transmit to their children only the nature that they themselves possess. Since every human parent has a sin nature, these parents transmit this same nature to their children. All people are born in sin. And what is sinful cannot enter the kingdom of God (John 3:5). The only way a person can enter God's forever family is to experience a spiritual rebirth, and that is precisely what Jesus emphasized to Nicodemus.

The moment we place our trust in Jesus, the Holy Spirit infuses our dead human spirits with the eternal life of God and we're reborn spiritually. *Is that not a great blessing?*

One moment we are spiritually dead; the next moment we are spiritually alive. At the moment of the new birth, the believer receives a new spiritual nature or capacity that expresses itself in spiritual concerns and interests. Whereas that person formerly was uninterested in the things of God, now (following the new birth) he becomes concerned with the things of God—His Word, His people, His service, His glory, and above all, God Himself.

I once had the opportunity of interviewing Charles Colson, a former "hatchet man" with the Nixon administration. Here was a man who formerly had no interest in the things of God. He was willing to sell out even his own grandmother if the occasion ever called for it.

Yet, following a series of horrible circumstances connected with the Watergate scandal of the Nixon years (including a stint in prison), Colson today is a different creature. He has been born again. His story may be found in his exciting book, *Born Again*. He presently heads Prison Fellowship, a wonderful ministry for prisoners across the United States. Formerly he had no interest in spiritual things; after his new birth, spiritual things became the dominant preoccupation of his life.

Like Colson, any person—regardless of background—can be born again. By simply trusting in Jesus, anyone can be born spiritually and enter into God's forever family. *Have you been born again?*

We Are Declared Righteous!

Humankind's dilemma of falling short of God's glory (Romans 3:23) pointed to the need for a solution. Man's sin—his utter unrighteousness—was such that there was no way he could come into a relationship with God on his own. Humankind was guilty before a holy God, and this guilt of sin put a barrier between man and God.

One of the wonderful blessings of salvation is that God solved this seemingly insurmountable problem by "declaring righteous" all those who believe in Jesus. Because of Christ's work on the cross—taking our place and bearing our sins— God acquits believers and pronounces a verdict of "not guilty."

Romans 3:24 tells us that God's declaration of righteousness is given to believers "freely by his grace." The word *grace* literally means "unmerited favor." It is because of God's unmerited favor that believers can freely be declared righteous before God.

But this doesn't mean God's declaration of righteousness has no objective basis. God didn't just subjectively decide to overlook man's sin or wink at his unrighteousness. Jesus died on the cross for us. He died in our stead. He paid for our sins. Jesus ransomed us from death by His own death on the cross.

There has been a great exchange. As the great Reformer Martin Luther said, "Lord Jesus, you are my righteousness, I am your sin. You have taken upon yourself what is mine and given me what is yours. You have become what You were not so that I might become what I was not."[1]

A key blessing that results from being declared righteous is that we now have peace with God (Romans 5:1). The Father sees believers through the lens of Jesus Christ. And because there is peace between the Father and Jesus Christ, there is also peace between the Father and believers who are in Christ.

If we were to look through a piece of red glass, everything would appear red. If we were to look through a piece of blue glass, everything would appear blue. If we were to look through a piece of yellow glass, everything would appear yellow, and so on.

Likewise, when we believe in Jesus Christ as our Savior, God looks at us *through the Lord Jesus Christ*. He sees us in all the white holiness of His Son. Our sins are imputed to the account of Christ and Christ's righteousness is imputed to our account. For this reason, the Scriptures say that there is now no condemnation—literally, *no punishment*—for those who are in Christ Jesus (Romans 8:1).

We Are Reconciled to God

Elizabeth Barrett Browning's parents disapproved so strongly of her marriage to Robert that they disowned her. Almost weekly, Elizabeth wrote love letters to her mother and father, asking for a reconciliation. They never once replied.

After ten years of letter writing, Elizabeth received a huge box in the mail. She opened it. To her dismay and heartbreak, the box contained all of her letters to her parents. Not one of them had ever been opened!

Today those love letters are among the most beautiful in classical English literature. Had her parents opened and read only a few of them, a reconciliation might have been effected.[2]

The Bible is God's letter of reconciliation to us. We should open and read it thoroughly and often.

It is noteworthy that there are two different New Testament Greek words for *reconciliation*. One word is used when two parties need to be reconciled; the other is used when only one party needs to be reconciled. In 2 Corinthians 5:19 the single-party word is used, for man needs to be reconciled to God. God has done nothing wrong, and so needs no reconciliation toward man.

By believing in Jesus, who paid for our sins at the cross, we are reconciled to God. And the alienation and estrangement that formerly existed is done away with.

We Are Forgiven

We all have seen and used those little electronic calculators. What happens if you make an error? You press the "clear" button and automatically the information you entered is eliminated from the calculator. Then you begin again, and there is no need to deal with your earlier mistake. In fact, there is no record of your mistake—it is lost forever![3]

That's what happens to our sins when God forgives us. The consequences may remain, but the guilt—the legal condemnation for the offense—is gone. This is one of the greatest blessings of salvation. *We are truly forgiven.*

Meditate upon the following verses and let them saturate your mind:

- God said, "Their sins and lawless acts I will remember no more" (Hebrews 10:17).

- Blessed is he whose transgressions are forgiven, whose sins are covered. Blessed is the man whose sin the LORD does not count against him and in whose spirit is no deceit (Psalm 32:1-2).

- You will again have compassion on us; you will tread our sins underfoot and hurl all our iniquities into the depths of the sea (Micah 7:19).

- As high as the heavens are above the earth, so great is his love for those who fear him; as far as the east is from the west, so far has he removed our transgressions from us (Psalm 103:11-12).

Look at that last verse again. There is a definite point that is north and another that is south—the North and South Poles. But there are no such points for east and west.

It doesn't matter how far you go to the east; you will never arrive where east begins because by definition east is the opposite of west. The two never meet. They never will meet and never could meet because they are defined as opposites.

To remove our sins "as far as the east is from the west" is by definition to put them where no one can ever find them. That is the forgiveness God has granted us.

Though it may be hard for us to understand, God is able to forget our past. God throws our sins into the depths of the sea and puts up a sign on the shore that reads, "No fishing."

Perhaps one of the best ways to illustrate how God has forever put away our sins is the apostle Paul's comments on the "certificate of debt" in Colossians 2:14. Back in ancient days, whenever someone was found guilty of a crime, the offender was put in jail and a certificate of debt was posted on the jail door. This certificate listed all the crimes the offender was found guilty of. Upon release, after serving the prescribed time in jail, the offender was given the certificate of debt, and on it was stamped "Paid in Full."

Well, Christ took the certificates of debt posted on each of our lives and nailed them to the cross. He paid for all our sins at the cross. Jesus' sacrifice paid in full the price for our sins. Interestingly, the phrase "It is finished," which Jesus uttered upon the cross when He completed the work of salvation (John 19:30), comes from the same Greek word translated "paid in full." *We are truly forgiven!*

We Are Adopted into God's Family

One of the greatest blessings of salvation is that believers are adopted into God's forever family. We become "sons of God" (Romans 8:14).

Being "sons of God" makes us members of God's family. And God adopts into His family *anyone* who believes in His Son, Jesus Christ. That is noticeably different from human adoptions, for human adults generally seek to adopt only the healthiest and best-behaved children. But *all* people are welcome in God's family.

Being adopted into God's family is a relationship of privilege and responsibility. As sons of God, we are called to live in a manner that reflects our new family relationship. We are called to reflect the family likeness (Matthew 5:48).

Contrary to the enslavement to sin that leads to fear, the believer has received the "Spirit of sonship" (Romans 8:15). The word "sonship" in that verse literally means "placing as a son."

This is significant, for in New Testament times an adopted son enjoyed all the rights and privileges of a natural-born son. Hence, we have no need to be fearful about approaching God. We can boldly approach His throne and say, "Abba, Father" (Romans 8:15). "Abba" is an Aramaic term of affection and intimacy—similar to the English word "daddy."

Because of this new relationship with God, believers are called "heirs of God" and "co-heirs with Christ" (Romans 8:17). In a typical family, each child receives a share in their parents' estate. This makes each child an heir, and the children as a group are coheirs. As God's children we are heirs, and collectively we are coheirs with Christ (Galatians 4:7).

We are also told in Scripture that believers inherit "every spiritual blessing" in Christ (Ephesians 1:3). And upon entering heaven, believers will inherit all the riches of God's glorious kingdom (1 Corinthians 3:21-23). *What a magnificent future awaits us!*

If you are a believer, you must never forget that your primary identity is that you are a member of God's forever family. This should affect your attitude, your behavior—everything in your life. Let your identity as a child of God be a source of strength and encouragement to you.

We Are Secure in Our Salvation

How horrible it would be if my children feared that I would kick them out of my family every time they did something wrong. Their lives would be plagued by fear. They would have no peace. Likewise, it would be horrible if you and I as Christians constantly feared being kicked out of God's family every time we did something wrong.

I believe that Scripture consistently teaches that once a person trusts in Christ and becomes a part of God's forever family, he or she is saved forever (Romans 8:28-30). No matter what that child of God does after the moment of salvation, he or she is saved.

Of course, as we noted in the previous chapter, that does not mean the Christian can get away with living in sin. If a child of God sins and refuses to repent, God brings discipline—sometimes very severe discipline—into his or her life to bring him or her to repentance (Hebrews 12:4-11). Christians will either respond to God's light or His heat.

Now, what are the scriptural evidences for our security in salvation? Ephesians 4:30 says that we are sealed unto the day of redemption by the Holy Spirit (*see also* Ephesians 1:13). This seal—which indicates ownership, authority, and security—cannot be broken. The seal guarantees our entry into heaven.

In addition, we are told that the Father keeps us in His sovereign hands, and no one can take us away from Him (John 10:28-30). God has us in His firm grip. And that grip will never let us go.

Not only that, but the Lord Jesus Himself regularly intercedes and prays for us (Hebrews 7:25). His work of intercession, as our divine High Priest, is necessary because of our weaknesses, our helplessness, and our immaturity as children of God. He knows our limitations, and He knows the power and strategy of the foe with whom we have to contend (Satan). He is therefore faithful in making intercession for us.

Jesus' care of Peter is an illustration of this truth. Jesus told Simon Peter, "Simon, Simon, Satan has asked to sift you as wheat. But I have prayed for you, Simon, that your faith may not fail. And when you have turned back, strengthen your brothers" (Luke 22:31-32).

Peter did fall into sin by denying Christ three times (Matthew 26:69-75). Satan really did a number on overconfident

Peter. But afterward, we see Jesus' prayer fulfilled. Peter's faith did not fail, and he went on to strengthen his brothers in the faith. Peter also ended up writing the biblical books 1 Peter and 2 Peter, which have greatly strengthened many generations of believers since his time.

Notice that Peter did not get kicked out of God's family for denying Jesus three times. He committed a bad sin. But Peter remained in God's family. Jesus knew what Peter was up against, and prayed for him accordingly. Jesus prays for you and me, too!

We Have a Defense Attorney

There is one final truth I want to share in this chapter—a truth closely related to Jesus' ministry of intercession on our behalf. And that is the wonderful truth that Jesus Himself is our advocate, our defense attorney. In 1 John 2:1-2 we read, "My dear children, I write this to you so that you will not sin. But if anybody does sin, we have one who speaks to the Father in our defense—Jesus Christ, the Righteous One. He is the atoning sacrifice for our sins, and not only for ours but also for the sins of the whole world."

Jesus is our defense attorney. A defense attorney becomes necessary when someone has been charged with a crime or a wrongdoing.

Who is our accuser? Scripture tells us it is Satan. In fact, in Revelation 12:10 Satan is called "the accuser of our brothers."

This is illustrated in the book of Job. Satan went before God's throne and brought accusations against Job (Job 1–3). Satan does that with us today as well. We can picture it this way:

Satan walks up to God (the Judge) and says, "God, how can you call Ron Rhodes a Christian? Did you see what he just did? He sinned! He's as fallen as they come!"

But at that moment, Jesus Christ—my defense attorney—steps up to God's throne and says, "Father, Ron Rhodes trusted me for salvation in 1971."

And the Father immediately says, "Case dismissed!"

Jesus is your defense attorney. Rejoice in this fact. Never forget it. He is on your side; and He will defend you.

Wondrous Blessings!

In view of the above, I think you'll agree with me that the blessings of salvation are truly wondrous. The moment a person believes in Jesus for salvation, he or she—

- is born spiritually

- is declared righteous

- is completely reconciled to God

- is forgiven of all sins

- is adopted into God's forever family

- is made eternally secure in his or her salvation

- and comes into a relationship with Jesus, who is our perpetual defender.

Is there not good reason to rejoice? Oh, the blessings of our salvation!

—∾— *A Verse to Hide in Your Heart* —∾—

"As high as the heavens are above the earth, so great is his love for those who fear him; as far as the east is from the west, so far has he removed our transgressions from us."

PSALM 103:11-12

Jesus Christ
The Heart of Your Salvation

Here are just a few of the blessings that accompany the salvation you have in Christ.

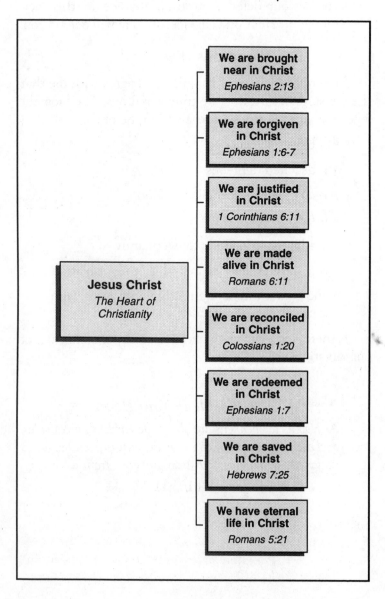

We are brought near in Christ
Ephesians 2:13

We are forgiven in Christ
Ephesians 1:6-7

We are justified in Christ
1 Corinthians 6:11

We are made alive in Christ
Romans 6:11

We are reconciled in Christ
Colossians 1:20

We are redeemed in Christ
Ephesians 1:7

We are saved in Christ
Hebrews 7:25

We have eternal life in Christ
Romans 5:21

Jesus Christ
The Heart of Christianity

> The goal of the Holy Spirit is to exalt and magnify the person of Jesus Christ in the lives of believers.

TEN

Power from On High: The Holy Spirit

In John's Gospel we find a touching account of Jesus with His disciples in the Upper Room (chapters 14–16). Jesus is soon to be crucified, and before His departure from them, He wanted to give them some final encouragements. One of these encouragements relates to the promise of the Holy Spirit.

In John 14:16 Jesus told the disciples, "I will ask the Father, and he will give you another Counselor to be with you forever." The word "counselor" is a rich one—carrying the meaning of "comforter, helper, advocate, one who strengthens." The concepts of encouragement, support, assistance, care, and the shouldering of responsibility for another's welfare are all conveyed by this one word.

It is interesting that there are two New Testament Greek words that can be translated into the English word "another." The first Greek word means "another of a *different* kind."

The second means "another of the *same* kind." It is the second word that is used in John 14:16.

Jesus was saying that He would ask the Father to send another Helper *of the same kind as Himself*—that is, a personal, ever-present helper. Just as Jesus was a personal comforter who helped the disciples for three years during His earthly ministry, so also would Christ's followers have another personal comforter—the Holy Spirit—who would be with them throughout their lives.

What a wonderful truth that is! We are never alone in our troubles. When life seems too much for us—when we encounter tough times or we're treated unfairly—we can rejoice in the presence of the Holy Spirit, who comforts, helps, and encourages us.

The Comforter Is a Person

Does it surprise you for me to say that the Holy Spirit is a person? Some people have assumed that the Holy Spirit is simply God's power or some kind of force that emanates from God. But the Scriptures portray the Holy Spirit as a person.

The Holy Spirit has all the attributes of personality. The three primary attributes of personality are mind, emotions, and will. A force does not have these attributes. But the Holy Spirit does. The Holy Spirit's intellect (or mind) is seen in 1 Corinthians 2:11, where we are told that the Holy Spirit knows the thoughts of God. That the Holy Spirit has emotions is clear from Ephesians 4:30, where we are admonished, "Do not grieve the Holy Spirit of God." The Holy Spirit's will is displayed in 1 Corinthians 12:11, where we are told that the Spirit distributes spiritual gifts "to each one, just as He determines."

The Holy Spirit's works confirm His personality. In Scripture, we see that the Holy Spirit does many things that only a person can do. For example, the Holy Spirit teaches believers (John 14:26), He testifies (John 15:26),

He guides (Romans 8:14), He commissions people to service (Acts 13:4), He issues commands (Acts 8:29), He prays for believers (Romans 8:26), and He speaks to people (2 Peter 1:21).

The Holy Spirit is treated as a person. Certain acts can be performed toward the Holy Spirit that would not make sense if He did not possess true personality. For example, a person can lie to the Holy Spirit (Acts 5:3). A person does not lie to a mere power. (Can you imagine how people might respond if I stood up in church one Sunday morning and confessed to lying to the electricity in my home?)

In view of the above—since the Holy Spirit has all the attributes of personality, does works only persons can do, and is treated as a person—we must conclude that indeed the Holy Spirit, the divine comforter, is truly a person.

The Comforter Is Truly God

Not only is the Holy Spirit a person, He is also God. He is just as much God as the Father and Jesus are. He is the third person of the holy Trinity.

How do we know the Holy Spirit is God? One reason is that the Holy Spirit is called God in the Bible (Acts 5:3-4). Beyond that, the Holy Spirit has all the attributes of God. For example, the Holy Spirit is *everywhere-present* (Psalm 139:7), *all-knowing* (1 Corinthians 2:10), *all-powerful* (Romans 15:19), *eternal* (Hebrews 9:14), and, of course, *holy* (John 16:7-14). Such attributes are possessed by God alone, and for the Holy Spirit to have them tells us He must be God.

Furthermore, the Holy Spirit performs works that only God can do. For example, He was involved in the work of creation (Genesis 1:2; Job 33:4; Psalm 104:30) and He inspired Scripture (2 Timothy 3:16; 2 Peter 1:21).

The Comforter Glorifies Christ

How does the Holy Spirit's ministry relate to Christ as the heart of Christianity? That is a very important question.

Scripture reveals that the primary purpose of the Holy Spirit is to bring glory to Jesus. Indeed, Jesus told the disciples in the Upper Room that the Holy Spirit would "bring glory to me by taking from what is mine and making it known to you" (John 16:14).

The goal of the Spirit, then, is not to make Himself prominent but to magnify and exalt the person of Jesus. He seeks to interpret and apply Jesus' teachings to His followers so that Jesus becomes central to their thinking and real in their lives. There's nothing that makes the Holy Spirit happier than for people to fall absolutely in love with Jesus and follow Him in all their ways.

We might say that the work of the Holy Spirit among believers is "Christocentric"—meaning that Christ is the very center of the Spirit's work among believers. Everything He does is related in some way to glorifying Christ. In all the Spirit's various ministries in the lives of believers, His ultimate goal is to glorify Jesus.

Marvelous Ministries of the Holy Spirit

The Scriptures tell us that the Holy Spirit is involved in a number of ministries among believers. Let's look at some of those ministries.

The Holy Spirit Seals Believers

The apostle Paul informs us that at the moment we believe in Jesus, we are "sealed for the day of redemption" (Ephesians 4:30). Indeed, we are marked "with a seal, the promised Holy Spirit" (1:13).

In ancient Rome, scrolls or documents sent from one location to another were sealed with wax that was imprinted with a Roman stamp. The authority of the Roman government protected that document against unauthorized opening. The seal could not be broken until the document reached its final destination.

In the same way, you and I as believers are sealed by the Holy Spirit for the day of redemption. We are sealed by God Himself. And that seal cannot be broken. This seal guarantees that you and I will be "delivered" into eternal life—on the "day of redemption." The Holy Spirit, as our seal, represents possession and security.

A similar type of seal is used in the trucking industry. For certain types of loads, a plastic seal is put around the lock on the back door of the truck. This seal cannot be broken before the truck reaches its destination. This is similar to the sealing of the Spirit. The seal of the Spirit cannot be broken before the Christian reaches his heavenly destination.

Notice in Ephesians 1:13 that the seal is also called a "mark" on the Christian. This mark stays with us, guaranteeing that we will enter heaven.

I used to live in Texas. Each spring the cattle ranchers round up all their one-year-old calves for branding. The brand is placed directly on the calf's flank. This is the rancher's mark of ownership. Once the brand is applied, no one can dispute that the calf belongs to him.

In the same way, God has placed His mark of ownership on us by the mark of the Holy Spirit. No one can remove us from His ownership anytime before the day of redemption.

The Holy Spirit Guides Believers

Another key ministry of the Holy Spirit is that He guides us. John 16:13 tells us that He guides us into all truth, and reveals the things of Christ to us.

We are not left to find our way alone. We are not abandoned to wander around in the darkness trying to find the light. We are not left to ourselves in our journey toward the promised land of heaven. The Holy Spirit is ever with us, guiding us along the way.

The following poem beautifully depicts this ministry of the Holy Spirit:

> Holy Spirit, faithful guide,
>   Ever near the Christian's side;
> Gently lead us by the hand,
>   Pilgrims in a desert land;
> Weary souls for e'er rejoice,
>   While they hear that sweetest voice
> Whisp'ring softly, wanderer, come!
>   Follow Me, I'll guide thee home.[1]

The Filling of the Holy Spirit

Every Christian is commanded to be filled with the Holy Spirit (Ephesians 5:18). And we are to continually *keep on being* filled by the Spirit. We know this because the word "filled" in Ephesians 5:18 is a present tense verb. That indicates continuing action. Day by day, moment by moment, you and I as Christians are to be filled with the Spirit. But what does that mean?

The context provides us with the answer. The verse says, "Do not get drunk on wine, which leads to debauchery. Instead, be filled with the Spirit" (Ephesians 5:18). Both drunk and Spirit-filled persons are *controlled* persons—that is, they're under the influence of either liquor or the Spirit and as a result they do things that are unnatural to them. In both cases they abandon themselves to an influence.

So, to be filled with the Holy Spirit means that we will be controlled or governed no longer by self but by the Holy Spirit. It is not a matter of acquiring more of the Spirit, but rather of the Spirit of God acquiring all of the individual.

A believer becomes filled with the Spirit when he or she is fully yielded to the indwelling Holy Spirit. This yieldedness results in a spiritual condition in which the Holy Spirit controls and empowers the individual moment by moment.

What exactly does it mean when we say a person is "filled"? A person "full of glee" is someone whose most dominant characteristic at the moment is glee. The person is yielded to gleefulness, and that gleefulness expresses itself in how he acts. A person "full of the Holy Spirit" is someone who is dominantly controlled by and surrendered to the Holy Spirit. And that person "full of the Holy Spirit" behaves in a way that's consistent with that filling. That is, the person acts in a way that is pleasing to God.

A.J. Gordon, one of the founders of Gordon Conwell Divinity School, said that one day he was out walking and looking across a field at a house. There beside the house was what looked like a man pumping furiously at a hand pump. As Gordon watched, the man continued to pump rapidly; he seemed absolutely tireless, pumping on and on, up and down, without ever slowing in the slightest.

It was truly a remarkable sight. So Gordon started to walk toward it. As he got closer, he could see that it was not a man at the pump, but a wooden figure painted to look like a man. The arm that was pumping so rapidly was hinged at the elbow and the hand was wired to the pump handle. The water was pouring forth, but not because the figure was pumping it. You see, it was an artesian well, and *the water was pumping the man!*[2]

When you see a person who is at work for God and producing spiritual results, you need to recognize that it is the Holy Spirit working through that person. Just as the wooden man was totally yielded to the water pump, so you and I as Christians need to be totally yielded to the Holy Spirit. When we are, we will produce results that are consistent with the will of God—and we will bring true glory to Christ.

Walking in the Spirit

Ever since Adam and Eve's fall into sin, all people have been born into the world with a sin nature. And this sin nature becomes manifest through numerous kinds of sin—covetousness, jealousy, dissension, bickering, and much more. In our own strength, we do not have the power to resist the evil inclinations of our sin nature. But we *can* have victory over the sin nature by walking in dependence upon the Holy Spirit. Galatians 5:16 tells us, "Live [or walk] by the Spirit, and you will not gratify the desires of the sinful nature."

In that verse, the word "live" (or walk) is a present tense verb, indicating continuing action. We are to persistently and continually walk in dependence upon the Spirit. As we do this, we will live in a way that is pleasing to God.

I read that at the close of World War II, two pictures showing a soldier in conflict with a tank appeared in a magazine. The first picture showed a huge tank bearing down on and about to crush a tiny soldier. The picture was proportioned to show the odds involved when a footsoldier with a rifle faced a tank.

The next picture showed what happened to that soldier's odds with a bazooka, or a rocket launcher, in his hands. This time the tank appeared to be shrunken in size and the soldier was much bigger.

Without the power of God released in our lives, we are like an infantry soldier in the presence of a tank when we try to confront our sin nature. We don't stand a chance against it. But by living and walking in the power of the Holy Spirit, we can say no to sin and enjoy victory over it. We can live as God intended us to live.

The Fruit of the Spirit

As we walk in dependence upon the Spirit, not only do we enjoy victory over sin, we also find the fruit of the Spirit being produced in our lives. Galatians 5:22-23 tells us that "the fruit of the Spirit is love, joy, peace, patience, kindness, goodness, faithfulness, gentleness and self-control."

Many theologians have noted that as we look at the qualities listed in Galatians 5:22-23, we find an accurate profile of Jesus Christ Himself. The character of our Lord is reproduced in our lives as we walk in dependence upon the Spirit. In this way, we progressively take on the family likeness (as members of God's forever family).

I once read a story about a slothful man who had moved into a new house. The house quickly began to show the effects of his slipshod lifestyle. The yard became littered with trash. The lawn withered for lack of care. The house was a wreck and was never cleaned.

Later, a young family bought the house and moved in. They painted the house, cleaned the yard, and replanted the lawn. The results were dramatic. What happened? There was a big improvement in the appearance of the house because there was a change of occupants in that house.

That's the way it is with a person who becomes a Christian and walks in dependence upon the Spirit. There is a dramatic change in that person's life because there is a perfect, new resident within—the Holy Spirit. And as we walk in dependence upon the Spirit, His fruit begins to grow in our lives.

Don't Grieve the Spirit

Closely related to walking in the Spirit is the instruction that we "not grieve the Holy Spirit of God" (Ephesians 4:30). In the original Greek text, this verse reads, "*Stop* grieving the Holy Spirit."

Is there a sin in your life that you fall into continually? If so, Scripture exhorts you to stop grieving the Holy Spirit and walk in dependence upon Him. If you do that, you will enjoy victory over the sin.

When the Spirit is grieved within a believer, the fellowship, guidance, instruction, and power of the Spirit are hindered. The Holy Spirit—though He still indwells the believer—is not free to accomplish His work. To grieve the Holy Spirit is to say good-bye to the fruit of the Spirit—such as love, joy, and peace. If these qualities are missing in your life, then consider the possibility that you may be doing something that grieves the Spirit.

The Holy Spirit Bestows Spiritual Gifts

One more ministry of the Holy Spirit I want to mention is that He bestows spiritual gifts upon believers (1 Corinthians 12:7,11). What are some of these gifts? The apostle Paul explains:

> We have different gifts, according to the grace given us. If a man's gift is prophesying, let him use it in proportion to his faith. If it is serving, let him serve; if it is teaching, let him teach; if it is encouraging, let him encourage; if it is contributing to the needs of others, let him give generously; if it is leadership, let him govern diligently; if it is showing mercy, let him do it cheerfully (Romans 12:6-8; *see* also 1 Corinthians 12:8-10)

We each have different spiritual gifts. But our gifts are to be used for the mutual benefit of the church, which is the body of Christ. I believe that my spiritual gift is the gift of teaching. I exercise this gift by writing books, speaking in churches and Bible schools, and much more. I discovered my gift as I became active in ministry in my church.

If you are unsure of what your spiritual gift is, the best advice I can give you is to get involved in the work of ministry at your local church. Your spiritual gift will surface as you serve in ministry.

Go ahead—contact someone on your church's pastoral staff and volunteer for a ministry. God will not only use you in ministry, but you will discover what your unique spiritual gift is!

There is so much more that could be said about the important ministries of the Holy Spirit in the believer's life, but space forbids. I hope this chapter has whetted your appetite to do more study on this fascinating doctrine.[3] What's important is that we remember this: One key to spiritual health in the life of the believer is a right relationship with the Holy Spirit.

Walk with Him. Your life will never be the same!

─ⵗ─ *A Verse to Hide in Your Heart* ─ⵗ─

"Live by the Spirit, and you will not gratify the desires of the sinful nature."

GALATIANS 5:16

> Jesus is our divine Shepherd. He guides and
> spiritually nourishes all who follow Him.

ELEVEN

Jesus, the Good Shepherd

There is much that could be said about Jesus' continuing ministry to us today. But the scriptural teaching that Jesus is our divine Shepherd is perhaps the most meaningful to me personally. I think the reason this aspect of Jesus' ministry touches me so deeply is that it is a perfect illustration of the intimate relationship that exists between Christ and His people.

In Scripture, Christ is called the Good Shepherd (John 10), the Chief Shepherd (1 Peter 5:3), and the Great Shepherd (Hebrews 13:20). In every way, Jesus is the ideal Shepherd for His people.

The Bible talks a lot about shepherds. Broadly speaking, Scripture indicates that the shepherd is simultaneously a leader and a companion to his sheep. He is a strong man capable of defending his flock against wild beasts (1 Samuel 17:34-37). He is also gentle with his flock, knowing their condition (Proverbs 27:23), bearing them in his arms (Isaiah

40:11), adapting himself to their needs (Genesis 33:13), and cherishing each and every one of them "like a daughter" (2 Samuel 12:3). The shepherd was known for seeking out lost sheep (Ezekiel 34:12) and for rescuing those that were attacked (Amos 3:12). In view of all that, the shepherd motif is certainly an appropriate way to describe the relationship Jesus has with His people.

PSALM 23

The LORD is my shepherd, I shall not be in want.

He makes me lie down in green pastures, he leads me beside quiet waters, he restores my soul. He guides me in paths of righteousness for his name's sake.

Even though I walk through the valley of the shadow of death, I will fear no evil, for you are with me; your rod and your staff, they comfort me.

You prepare a table before me in the presence of my enemies. You anoint my head with oil; my cup overflows.

Surely goodness and love will follow me all the days of my life, and I will dwell in the house of the LORD forever.

"Three thousand years have passed since the psalmist David first sang the words of the Twenty-third Psalm," says theologian Haddon Robinson in his inspirational book on Psalm 23. He adds:

The sand of those thirty centuries has buried beneath it many of the relics of that distant day. The harp on which this ancient melody was played, the book of the law from which King David drew his meditations, the royal chamber in which the psalmist composed his song, are now all covered with the debris of the ages. Yet, the Twenty-third Psalm is still as fresh as the day it was first composed.[1]

David, once a shepherd himself who went to great lengths to care for his sheep, reflects in Psalm 23 on how God has taken care of him. Inspired by the Spirit, David exulted, "The LORD is my shepherd..."

Jesus Provides for Every Need

David learned by experience that because the Lord was his shepherd, all of his needs would be fully met. And David was fully satisfied with the Lord's management of his life.

David believed that the Lord had planned his life down to the details of his day, as a good shepherd would. It was in the knowledge that the Lord was at the helm of his life that David went about his days in joy, believing that any trials that came his way were taking place within the Lord's sovereign plan. Moreover, whenever a difficult circumstance did come up, David could rest assured that the Lord was with him every minute.

In his affirmation that the Lord was his shepherd, David was likening himself to a sheep. Sheep are defenseless, dependent, and foolish animals. So David was acknowledging in Psalm 23 that he was utterly dependent upon the Lord. And he trusted the Lord to defend him against trouble.

David said that because the Lord was his shepherd, "I shall not be in want." This phrase carries the meaning, "Because the Lord is my shepherd, I shall never be in a state of lack at any time for anything I need."

Thoughtful Christians have pointed out that we must be careful not to get sidetracked so that our focus is merely on the benefits of following the Shepherd. Rather, our focus must ever be on the Shepherd Himself; then, all else will follow. Haddon Robinson comments,

Sometimes we get so taken up with the details of this psalm that we actually ignore the Shepherd. We are delighted at the prospect of green pastures and quiet waters. We respond to the promise of an overflowing cup. Indeed, we are so eager for all the Shepherd does, we do not pay much attention to who the Shepherd is. Yet He is at the center of the entire psalm. All of these blessings are mine because I am one of His sheep.[2]

Jesus Nourishes Us Spiritually

David said of the Lord, "He makes me lie down in green pastures, he leads me beside quiet waters, he restores my soul. He guides me in paths of righteousness for his name's sake" (Psalm 23:2-3).

Just as a shepherd leads his sheep to green pastures and quiet waters, so also does the Lord give us spiritual nourishment and refreshment. When we have put our affairs in the hands of the Lord, then, we will know contentment.

It is significant that the phrase "quiet waters" can be translated "stilled waters." As in most of Psalm 23, David is thinking of what a shepherd faces in the course of his work.

You see, sheep are deeply afraid of running water. By instinct they seem to realize that if water should get on their wool coats, they would become waterlogged and sink into the water. Because of this, a flock that is tired and thirsty will come to a running stream and then stand beside it and look. Fear keeps them from partaking of the refreshing waters.[3]

Aware of this fear, the shepherd—perhaps taking his rod and staff—might pry loose a few large stones to dam up a quiet place where the sheep may drink. In the midst of a rushing stream, he creates a place of still water and provides refreshment for the flock.

A good shepherd in the Near East will go to no end of trouble to supply his sheep with the finest grazing, the richest pasturage, and the cleanest water. He does everything in his power to ensure the highest possible quality of life for them. Likewise, our Shepherd Jesus always makes sure that those who follow Him stay spiritually nourished and refreshed.

Throughout Scripture, the drinking of water is often used to show spiritual refreshment. For example, Jesus told the woman at the well in Samaria that He could give her "living water" (John 4:10). Jesus informed her that "whoever drinks the water I give him will never thirst. Indeed, the water I give him will become in him a spring of water welling up to eternal life" (verse 14).

Later in John's Gospel we read that "on the last and greatest day of the Feast, Jesus stood and said in a loud voice, 'If anyone is thirsty, let him come to me and drink. Whoever believes in me, as the Scripture has said, streams of living water will flow from within him'" (John 7:37-38).

Clearly, the goal of Jesus our Shepherd is that we might be spiritually nourished and have life more abundantly. But there is a "catch" of sorts: Christ does not insist on imposing Himself upon us and forcing us to follow His lead. He does not override our wills. He does not rush into our daily experiences and gate-crash His way into our lives. Having made us in His own likeness—as free-will agents able to choose to do as we wish—it is ultimately up to us to follow His lead. That is an important choice facing each of us.

If we choose to follow Christ's lead, we will find our souls refreshed and guided in paths of righteousness for His name's sake (Psalm 23:3). Christ our Shepherd will never lead us astray or on the wrong path. His paths lead to spiritual nourishment and refreshment.

If we find ourselves in a barren wasteland spiritually, it is not because He has led us there, but because we have chosen to stop following His lead. Without a conscientious effort to stay close to our divine Shepherd, we will likely end up somewhere out in the desert of life, torn and bleeding—like the unfortunate Israelites in their wilderness experience.

Perhaps even now you may feel that your spiritual life has been stagnating in a dry wasteland. If so, take heart, for your Shepherd seeks your full restoration. His arms are opened wide, waiting to embrace you in unconditional love. His affection is as measureless as the sea. Turn to Him without delay, and you will be able to say with David, "The LORD is my shepherd, I shall not be in want" (Psalm 23:1).

Jesus Walks With Us in Tough Times

David said, "Even though I walk through the valley of the shadow of death, I will fear no evil, for you are with me; your rod and your staff, they comfort me" (Psalm 23:4).

Bible scholars believe the "valley of the shadow of death" refers to a treacherous, dreadful place. In fact, the phrase is probably better translated "the valley of deep darkness." It may be that the psalmist is thinking of an actual place in Palestine—a chasm among the hills or a deep, abrupt, faintly lighted ravine with steep sides and a narrow floor. This place is a home for vultures by day and a haven for wolves and hyenas by night. The danger for defenseless sheep is obvious.

Because the Lord is with him, David fears no evil while passing through this dreadful valley. The truth we learn from this is that no matter what dark circumstances we might find ourselves passing through, Christ our Shepherd is with us and we need not ever fear.

What did David mean when he said, "Your rod and your staff, they comfort me"? The shepherd's rod is a great oak club about two feet long. It had a round head in which the shepherd had pounded sharp bits of metal. This rod was used to protect the sheep from wild animals.

The staff was bent or hooked at one end. It was often used by shepherds to restrain a sheep from wandering or to hook its legs to pull it out of a hole into which it had fallen. At other times, the shepherd would use the staff to pull aside branches when a sheep got entangled in brush.

By using the rod and the staff, the shepherd brought comfort to his sheep. In Psalm 23:4, the Hebrew word for "comfort" literally means "to give strength" or "empower." In the presence of their shepherd, the sheep were strengthened and empowered because they knew they were secure.

The same is true of us as Christ's sheep. Knowing that He is with us every step of the way, gives us strength to cope with whatever might come. Believers are never in situations the Lord is not aware of, and He never forsakes His people (Hebrews 13:5).

Jesus Refreshes and Restores Us

David said of the Lord, "You prepare a table before me in the presence of my enemies. You anoint my head with oil; my cup overflows" (Psalm 23:5).

This verse tells us that those who follow the Shepherd are well-fed and well-nourished. If any sheep in Christ's flock find themselves in a spiritual wasteland, it is because they have strayed from the Shepherd's side. Those who follow the Lord closely will never find themselves in such a spiritual environment.

A shepherd in the ancient Near East would often pick a branch off a tree and, as he walked, hold the branch behind him so that sheep could follow closely and nibble on the morsels. This illustrates a profound truth for us: *Those who stay nearest the shepherd are the best nourished.*

The same is true of us. Those of us who stay nearest to our divine Shepherd are the best nourished spiritually and the most refreshed in our inner being. Those who walk with Jesus the Shepherd will find their strength continually renewed.

Jesus Brings Goodness

David closes this marvelous psalm by affirming, "Surely goodness and love will follow me all the days of my life, and I will dwell in the house of the LORD forever" (Psalm 23:6).

David recognized that with all that was true about the divine Shepherd, surely only goodness and love would prevail in his life. How could it be otherwise? For the Shepherd Himself is utterly good and loving. Those who stay near Him therefore find themselves showered with His goodness and love.

David also affirmed that he would dwell in the house of the Lord forever. David's commitment was not a fleeting one; he was unreservedly committed—forever.

In Psalm 23, we learn an important lesson from David. We can intellectually know that the Lord is a Shepherd, but that knowledge in itself will not do us much good. We can intellectually understand that the Lord, if permitted, is capable of meeting our needs. But it is only when we come before Him and place our lives completely in His hands and say, "The Lord is *my* Shepherd" that the blessings in this psalm will become real in our lives. Only when we truly make the Lord our Shepherd with a fully committed heart will we be able to say along with David that "I shall not be in want."

Praise to Christ Our Shepherd

In Psalm 23 we have seen that our divine Shepherd is with us at every moment. He intimately cares about even the smallest details of our lives. He leads and guides us, protects us, spiritually nourishes and refreshes us, gives us abundant life, provides for all our needs, comforts us during tough times, and bestows goodness and love upon us. Christ the divine Shepherd did all that among the people of God in Bible times, and He does all that for us today as well. *Praise be to our Great Shepherd!*

Remember, Christ Himself is the Creator of the entire universe and sustains it by the word of His power (Colossians 1:16). Isn't it amazing to ponder that this same glorious being has become *our* Shepherd.

Real-life shepherd Phillip Keller reflects,

> All this is a bit humbling. It drains the "ego" from a man and puts things in proper perspective. It makes me see myself as a mere mite of material in an enormous universe. Yet the staggering fact remains that Christ the Creator of such an enormous universe of overwhelming magnitude, deigns to call Himself my Shepherd and invites me to consider myself His sheep— His special object of affection and attention. Who better could care for me?[4]

Christ wants to be *your* Shepherd. In Psalm 23, it's as if He's saying to you, "Entrust the keeping of your soul and life to Me. Let Me lead you gently in the paths of righteousness and peace. My part is to show the way. Your part is to walk in it. All will be well."[5]

～ *A Verse to Hide in Your Heart* ～

"The LORD is my shepherd, I shall not be in want."

PSALM 23:1

> Three ingredients that help us grow in our
> relationship with the Lord are prayer, walk-
> ing by faith, and reading God's Word.

TWELVE

Ingredients for a Healthy Spiritual Life

I'm not much of a cook. But one thing I've learned from watching other people cook is that if you leave a key ingredient out of a recipe, it's not going to turn out right.

Though there are many ingredients to a healthy spiritual life, I think there are three that are especially important. These are prayer, living by faith, and reading God's Word. If any of these key ingredients is missing, our spiritual growth will turn just as sour as a recipe missing a key ingredient. These three are absolutely foundational to a healthy spiritual life.

Communication Through Prayer

George Müller was a man who had many orphans under his care; too many, in fact, for himself to support financially without God's intervention. One morning at his orphanage the tables were all set for breakfast, but the cupboard was completely bare. There was no food, and there was no money!

While the children stood around waiting for their breakfasts, Mr. Müller said to them, "Children, you know we must be in time for school." He then lifted his head and prayed, "Dear Father, we thank Thee for what Thou art going to give us to eat."

Almost immediately after this, there was a knock at the door. It was a local baker. He said, "Mr. Müller, I could not sleep last night. Somehow I felt you didn't have any bread for breakfast, and the Lord wanted me to send you some. So I got up at 2:00 A.M. and baked some fresh bread and here it is." Mr. Müller humbly thanked the baker and then offered praise to God for providing so miraculously for him and the orphans.

Moments later there was a second knock at the door. It was the local milkman, whose wagon had just broken down in front of Müller's orphanage. He offered all his milk to Müller and the orphans so he could have his wagon hauled to the nearest repair shop.[1] Coincidence? I don't think so!

While I've never had as immediate and incredible an answer to prayer as George Müller did, I *have* had many prayers answered through the years. I've seen with my own eyes that prayer works. And God wants *you* to know that prayer works. Let's consider a few important verses.

Ask and It Will Be Given

One Bible passage that came to my mind when I read Müller's account was Matthew 7:7-8, in which Jesus said, "Ask and it will be given to you; seek and you will find; knock and the door will be opened to you. For everyone who asks receives; he who seeks finds; and to him who knocks, the door will be opened." *Müller asked and it was given.*

Müller, in his unique situation, received an instant answer and only had to ask once—and we can be thankful for occasions like that. But I need to point out that the tenses in the Greek text of Matthew 7:7-8 actually carry the idea, "*Keep on* asking and it will be given; *keep on* seeking and you will find; *keep on* knocking and the door will be opened." This verse explicitly tells us not to give up in prayer. We need to hang in there.

The reason I bring that up is that sometimes Christians get discouraged if they don't get an immediate answer to prayer. Also, some Christians think that if they have to make the same request more than one time, then perhaps they aren't praying with enough faith. But that is not the teaching of Scripture. We are to keep on asking, keep on seeking, keep on knocking. Never give up on prayer; God will answer.

Entrusting Problems into God's Care

I remember when I was young my sister was given a plastic doll. She played with it day in and day out. Eventually one of the arms broke off. My sister promptly went to my dad and asked him to fix it. My dad was glad to do it, but my sister didn't want to let go of the doll. She wanted to keep holding on to it. That prevented my father from fixing it.

Soon after, the other arm broke off. Again my sister went to my dad, but she didn't want to let go of the doll. Again my father was prevented from fixing it.

Well, later on both of the legs popped off too, and by this time my sister was getting desperate. So finally, mustering all her strength of will, she surrendered the broken mess to my father. Within minutes my dad had the doll reassembled and good as new.

Sometimes we are that way with God. We go to God in prayer about a matter, but we don't really entrust the entire situation to Him. We hold on to it, fret about it, and try to solve the problem in our own strength. Often we wait until things get desperately bad before we finally turn to God and release everything into His care. How much wiser it would be to turn every problem over to Him the moment it arises!

The Scriptures instruct us, "Do not be anxious about anything, but in everything, by prayer and petition, with thanksgiving, present your requests to God. And the peace of God, which transcends all understanding, will guard your hearts and your minds in Christ Jesus" (Philippians 4:6-7). No problem is too small or too big to entrust into God's care.

Prayer God's Way

Though space forbids a more detailed treatment of prayer in this chapter, there are a few brief insights I definitely want to mention. These are especially important:

• We must remember that all our prayers are subject to the sovereign will of God. If we ask for something God doesn't want us to have, He will sovereignly deny that request. First John 5:14 tells us, "This is the confidence we have in approaching God: that if we ask anything *according to his will*, he hears us" (emphasis added).

• Prayer should not be an occasional practice but rather a continual one. We are instructed in 1 Thessalonians 5:17 to "pray continually." Prayer should be a daily habit.

• Recognize that sin hinders God from answering our prayers. Psalm 66:18 says, "If I had cherished sin in my heart, the Lord would not have listened."

• Living righteously, on the other hand, is a great benefit to getting prayers answered. Proverbs 15:29 says, "The LORD is far from the wicked but he hears the prayer of the righteous."

• A good model prayer is the Lord's Prayer found in Matthew 6:9-13. In this one prayer we find praise (verse 9), personal requests (verses 11-13), and an affirmation of God's will (verse 10).

The Eye of Faith

It was a Wednesday afternoon. Shrouded in a dense fog, a large steamer edged slowly forward off the coast of Newfoundland, its foghorn crying out somber notes of warning. The captain—near exhaustion from lack of sleep—was startled by a gentle tap on his shoulder. He turned and found himself face-to-face with an old man in his late seventies.

The old man said, "Captain, I have come to tell you that I must be in Quebec on Saturday afternoon."

The captain pondered for a moment, and then snorted, "Impossible."

"Very well," the old man responded, "if your ship can't take me, God will find some other means to take me. I have never broken an engagement in 57 years."

Lifting his weary hands in a gesture of despair, the captain replied, "I would help if I could—but I am helpless."

Undaunted, the old man suggested, "Let's go down to the chart room and pray." The captain raised his eyebrows in utter disbelief, looking at the old man as if he had just escaped from a lunatic asylum.

"Do you know how dense the fog is?" the captain demanded.

The old man responded, "No. My eye is not on the thickness of the fog but on the living God who controls every circumstance of my life."

Against his better judgment, the captain accompanied the old man to the chart room and kneeled with him in prayer. With simple words a child might use, the old man prayed, "O Lord, if it is consistent with Thy will, please remove this fog in five minutes. Thou knowest the engagement Thou didst make for me in Quebec on Saturday. I believe it is Thy will."

The captain, a nominal Christian at best, thought it wise to humor the old man and recite a short prayer. But before he was able to utter a single word, he felt a tap on his shoulder. The old man requested, "Don't pray, because you do not believe; and as I believe God has already answered, there is no need for you to pray." The captain's mouth dropped open.

Then the old man explained, "Captain, I have known my Lord for 57 years and there has never been a single day that I have failed to gain an audience with the King. Get up, captain, and open the door, and you will find the fog is gone." The captain did as he was requested, and was astonished to find that the fog had indeed disappeared.

The captain later testified that this encounter with the aged George Müller completely revolutionized his Christian life. He had seen with his own eyes that Müller's God was the true and living God of the Bible. He had seen incredible power flow from a frail old man—a power rooted in simple childlike faith in God.[2]

Pastor Ray Stedman once delivered a sermon in which he said, "Faith has an apparent ridiculousness about it. You are not acting by faith if you are doing what everyone around you is doing. Faith always appears to defy the circumstances. It constitutes a risk and a venture."[3]

That is the kind of faith George Müller demonstrated decade after decade in his long and fruitful life. During the final year of his earthly sojourn, he wrote that his faith had been increasing over the years little by little, but he emphatically insisted that *there was nothing unique about him or his faith*. He believed that a life of trust was open to virtually all of God's children if only they would endure when trials came instead of giving up.

Perceiving Unseen Realities

The apostle Paul defines faith as "being sure of what we hope for and certain of what we do not see" (Hebrews 11:1). I like John Wesley's paraphrase of this verse: "Faith is the power to see into the world of spirits, into things invisible and eternal. It is the power to understand those things which are not perceived by worldly senses."[4]

Of course, the big problem for most of us is that we tend to base everything on what our five senses tell us. And since the spiritual world is not subject to any of these, our faith is often weak and impotent.

Devotional writer A.W. Tozer analyzed the problem this way:

> The world of sense intrudes upon our attention day and night for the whole of our lifetime. It is clamorous, insistent, and self-demonstrating. It does not appeal to our faith; it is here, assaulting our five senses, demanding to be accepted as real and final. But sin has so clouded the lenses of our hearts that we cannot see that other reality, the City of God, shining around us. The world of sense triumphs.[5]

The eye of faith, however, perceives this unseen reality. The spiritual world lies all about us, enclosing us, embracing us, altogether within our reach. God Himself is here awaiting our response to His presence. This spiritual world will come alive to us the moment we begin to reckon upon its reality.

Do you know the story of Elisha in 2 Kings 6:8-23? Elisha found himself in a situation where he was completely surrounded by enemy troops, yet he remained calm and relaxed. His servant, however, must have been distressed at the sight of this hostile army with vicious-looking warriors and innumerable battle chariots on every side.

Undaunted, Elisha said to him, "Don't be afraid.... Those who are with us are more than those who are with them" (2 Kings 6:16). Elisha then prayed to God, "'O LORD, open his eyes so he may see.' Then the LORD opened the servant's eyes, and he looked and saw the hills full of horses and chariots of fire all around Elisha" (2 Kings 6:17).

God was protecting Elisha and his servant with a whole army of magnificent angelic beings!

The reason Elisha never became worried was because he was "sure of what he hoped for and certain of what [he did] not see" (Hebrews 11:1). The eye of faith recognizes that God acts on our behalf even when we don't perceive it with our physical senses.

Faith in God Alone

The object of a Christian's faith is not his or her own abilities or the finite strength of man. *The object of a believer's faith is the all-powerful God.*

Consider the story of David and Goliath. Humanly speaking, David had no chance of conquering the mighty giant who had been arrogantly defying the armies of Israel. But David, looking at the situation through the eye of faith, could perceive the unseen divine forces that were fighting on his side.

Saul—who was blind to all of this—warned David, "You are not able to go out against this Philistine and fight him; you are only a boy, and he has been a fighting man from his youth" (1 Samuel 17:33).

But David asserted, "The LORD who delivered me from the paw of the lion and the paw of the bear will deliver me from the hand of this Philistine" (1 Samuel 17:37).

Then, when David came face to face with the giant warrior, he declared, "This day the LORD will hand you over to me, and I'll strike you down....the battle is the LORD's, and he will give all of you into our hands" (1 Samuel 17:46-47).

The rest is history. Goliath lost the fight before it had even begun. Why? Because the object of David's faith was a mighty God who once declared, "I am the LORD, the God of all mankind. Is anything too hard for me?" (Jeremiah 32:27).

The eye of faith does not focus on human weakness and inability. Rather, it is focused solely on the Deliverer—the Lord Himself.

Conditioning the Faith Muscle

I've always been taught that faith is like a muscle. A muscle has to be repeatedly stretched to its limit of endurance to build more strength. Without increased stress in training, the muscle simply will not grow.

In the same way, faith must be repeatedly tested to the limit of its endurance so it can expand and develop. Very often, God allows His children to go through trying experiences to develop their faith muscles.

This principle is beautifully illustrated in the book of Exodus. Following Israel's deliverance from Egypt, God first led the people to Marah, a place where they would have to trust Him to heal the water so that it was drinkable (Exodus 15:22-26). It is significant that God led the Israelites to Marah before leading them to Elim, a gorgeous oasis with plenty of good water (verse 27). God could have bypassed Marah altogether and brought the people directly to Elim if He had wanted to. But, as is characteristic of God, He purposefully led them through the route that would yield maximum conditioning of their faith muscles.

Likewise, God often governs our circumstances so as to permit maximum conditioning of our faith muscles.

Faith and the Word of God

The great Reformer John Calvin once said that "we must be reminded that there is a permanent relationship between faith and the Word. God could not separate one from the other any more than we could separate the rays from the sun from which they come."[6] Indeed, God's Word "is the basis whereby faith is supported and sustained; if it turns away from the Word, it falls. Therefore, take away the Word and no faith will then remain."[7]

The New Testament writers were adamant on this issue. John's Gospel tells us that "these [things] are written that you may believe" (John 20:31). Paul says that "faith comes from hearing the message, and the message is heard through the word of Christ" (Romans 10:17). If someone should ask, "How can I increase my faith?" the answer is: *Saturate your mind with God's Word.*

In this chapter we have looked at some inspiring examples of how George Müller's faith and prayer life reaped incredible results. It is no surprise that Müller saw a cause-and-effect relationship between God's Word and faith. Based on what he learned over the years, he offered two suggestions for Christians who want to see powerful results from their faith.

First, since true faith is solidly anchored upon scriptural facts, we must not allow ourselves to be influenced by emotional impressions. "Impressions have neither one thing nor the other to do with faith," says Müller. "Faith has to do with the Word of God. It is not impressions, strong or weak, which will make the difference. We have to do with the Written Word and not ourselves or impressions."[8] (If Müller had based his outlook on mere impressions, he would have given up trying to get to Quebec on time through the thick fog.)

And second, we must beware of letting probabilities hinder our faith. Müller warns, "Many people are willing to believe regarding those things that seem probable to them. Faith has nothing to do with probabilities. The province of faith begins where probabilities cease and sight and sense fail. Appearances are not to be taken into account. The question is—whether God has spoken it in His Word."[9] (If Müller had based his outlook on mere probabilities, then he and the children at his orphanage would have gone hungry on that fateful morning.)

Like Müller, we must feed daily on the Word of God. If we do this, we will find our faith growing day by day.

Recipe for Spiritual Growth

Prayer, walking by faith, and reading God's Word—these are three of the key ingredients in the recipe for spiritual growth.

When you think about it, all of the spiritual giants mentioned in the Bible were characterized by prayer, walking by faith, and being strong in the Word. Not only that, all the great saints that God has used throughout church history have been characterized by these three ingredients.

Let's imitate their example.

If we do, we'll find our personal relationship with the Lord Jesus soaring to ever new heights of intimacy.

—⁓— *A Verse to Hide in Your Heart* —⁓—

*"Do not be anxious about anything, but in everything,
by prayer and petition, with thanksgiving, present your
requests to God. And the peace of God, which transcends
all understanding, will guard your hearts
and your minds in Christ Jesus."*

PHILIPPIANS 4:6-7

> The three primary enemies of the Christian
> are the world, the flesh, and the Devil.
> Christ gives us victory.

THIRTEEN

Winning Battles

I wish I could tell you that from the moment you become a Christian everything afterward will be smooth sailing. But the reality is that there are three potent enemies aligned against those who seek to walk with Christ—the world, the flesh, and the devil. Each of these work in concert with the others to bring about the downfall of the Christian.

Military strategists have long recognized that a large part of defeating the enemy is *knowing* the enemy. Only those who know the strategies of their opponents stand a chance of defeating them.

It is critical for the Christian to recognize that this destructive trio does not fight fair. It is a gang attack. No matter where we go in the world, we are engaged in spiritual combat. There is no spiritual demilitarized zone. The whole planet is a battleground. For this reason, this chapter will focus on these three enemies of the Christian. Prepare for battle!

Enemy #1: The World

I read a story about a flock of wild geese that was flying south for the winter. As they were traveling, one of the geese looked down and noticed a group of domestic geese by a pond on a farm. He saw that they had plenty of grain to eat, so he went down to join them. The food was so good, he decided to stay with the domestic geese until spring, when his own flock would fly north again.

When spring came, he heard his old flock going by and flew up to join them. The goose had grown fat, however, and flying was difficult. So he decided to spend one more season on the farm and join the wild geese on their next winter migration.

The following fall, when his former flock flew southward, the goose flapped his wings a little, but kept eating his grain. And by the time they passed overhead yet again, the now-domesticated goose didn't even notice them.[1]

This illustrates what can happen to the Christian in the "world." The Christian can slowly become so comfortable in the world system that he or she loses sight or even loses interest in his or her true calling and life as a Christian.

In Scripture, the word *world* often refers not to the physical planet (earth) but to *an anti-God system headed by Satan.* Indeed, 1 John 5:19 tells us that "the whole world is under the control of the evil one [Satan]." (Throughout the rest of this chapter I'll use the word *world* in this sense.)

Before we were Christians, you and I followed the ways of the world without hesitation (Ephesians 2:2). But when we became Christians, we changed over to another master—Jesus Christ—who calls us to be separate from the world.

The world is portrayed in Scripture as a seducer. It perpetually seeks to attract our attention and devotion away from God. It seeks to eclipse our view of heavenly things. It can subtly trap us and lead us astray. For this reason the New Testament instructs us not to love the world or anything in it (1 John 2:15-16).

There are many things in the world that appeal to our sin nature. If we give in to these, our attention is drawn away from God. Embracing the world and its ways will inevitably drive our affections away from God. *There is no neutral ground.*

What are some of the lures of the world that may entice us away from God? We may be enticed by money, material possessions, fame, a career, entertainment, pleasure, or any number of other things. These things are not necessarily wrong or evil in themselves; but used wrongly, they have the potential to shift our attention away from Christ as our first priority. Any of these can effectively sidetrack us into the web of worldliness.

I use the word web purposefully: Sometimes I come across a spider web with an insect stuck in its grasp. This makes it easy for the spider to move in for the kill. In a way, the world system is like a web that seeks to entrap us. This web makes it easy for Satan to move in and harm us.

Enemy #2: The Flesh

Another subtle enemy of the Christian is the *flesh*. The Bible uses the term *flesh* to describe that force within each of us that is in total rebellion against God. This "sin nature" was not a part of man when God originally created him. Rather, it entered Adam and Eve the moment they disobeyed God and He withdrew His spiritual life from them. Since the time of Adam and Eve, all people have been born into the world with a flesh nature or sin nature that rebels against God.

What are some manifestations of the flesh? Scripture tells us that the flesh in each of us gives rise to things like hatred, discord, jealousy, fits of rage, selfish ambition, dissensions, factions, envy, drunkenness, and the like (Galatians 5:20-21). These kinds of things greatly hinder our relationship with God.

It is critical to understand that when you and I become Christians, the flesh or sin nature in us is not done away with. It stays with us until we receive our transformed resurrection bodies in the future. Until that day, the flesh is ever-present.

The good news is that the *power* of the flesh to operate in the life of the Christian has been effectively neutralized by virtue of our being united with Christ in His death to sin. The flesh no longer has the right to reign in the Christian's life, and its power is broken in our lives when we—by faith—count this as being true (Romans 6:1-14).

The story is told of Handley Page, a pioneer in aviation, who once landed in an isolated area during his travels. Unknown to him, a rat got on board the plane there. On the next leg of his flight, Page heard the sickening sound of gnawing. Suspecting it was a rodent, his heart began to pound as he visualized the serious damage that could be done to the fragile mechanisms that controlled his plane. Such damage would be extremely difficult and expensive to repair.

What could he do? He remembered hearing that a rat cannot survive at high altitudes. So he pulled back on the stick. The airplane climbed higher and higher until Page himself found it difficult to breathe.

He listened intently and finally sighed with relief. The gnawing had stopped. And when he arrived at his destination, he found the rat lying dead behind the cockpit![2]

Often we, as God's children, are plagued by sin that gnaws at our lives simply because we are living at too low a spiritual level. To see sin defeated in our lives requires that we move up away from the world to a higher level where the things of this world cannot survive. By faith we need to count on the power of sin being broken in our lives by virtue of our spiritual union with Jesus Christ. He gives us the victory; keep your eyes on Him!

As well, we need to walk in the power of the Holy Spirit (Galatians 5:16). To walk in the Spirit means to have a continuing attitude of dependence upon the Spirit and not on our own human resources. As we walk in dependence upon Him, the power of the flesh is rendered inoperative. But if we walk in our own strength, the flesh will surely gain the upper hand.

Let us never make the mistake of thinking that just because we have become Christians, and we've enjoyed a few spiritual "highs" with the Lord, we have become immune to the sins of the flesh. Nothing could be further from the truth. The fact is, a true Christian can and does experience fleshly sins and will do so for as long as he is on this earth.

However, a true Christian will always have a desire to be delivered from these sins for the sake of his or her relationship with Christ. Because the Holy Spirit dwells inside of the Christian, he or she can't be *continually* happy in sin. Sooner or later the Christian will acknowledge his sin and turn back to trusting Christ to deliver him from its power.

There's one more point I need to make here: *It is not a sin to be tempted* to commit a sin of the flesh. All of us are tempted. But the temptation does not become sin unless we give in to it.

There's an old saying: "You can't stop a bird from landing on your head, but you can stop it from building a nest in your hair." We can't keep from being tempted, but we can prevent that temptation from taking root in our heart and giving rise to sin.

Enemy #3: The Devil

A third enemy of the Christian is the devil and his horde of fallen angels (also called demons). Satan, the devil, is pictured in Scripture as being extremely influential in the world. He is called "the prince of this world" (John 12:31) and "the god of this age" (2 Corinthians 4:4). He is also said to deceive the whole world (Revelation 12:9; 20:3).

How Scripture Speaks About Satan

It is fascinating to study the various ways the Bible speaks about Satan. Indeed, we learn much about Satan and his work by the various names and titles used of him. For example:

• Satan is called *the accuser of the brethren* (Revelation 12:10). Accusing God's people is a continuous, ongoing work of Satan. He never lets up. This verse tells us that Satan accuses God's people "day and night." Satan opposes God's people in two ways. First, he brings charges against believers before God (Zechariah 3:1). Second, he accuses believers to their own conscience.

• Satan is called *the devil* (Matthew 4:1). This word carries the idea of "adversary." The devil was and is the adversary of Christ and all who follow Christ.

• Satan is called our *enemy* (Matthew 13:39). The Greek word used here comes from a root word meaning "hatred." It characterizes Satan's attitude in an absolute sense. He hates both God and His children.

• Satan is called *the evil one* (1 John 5:19). He is the opposer of all that is good and the promoter of all that is evil. He is the very embodiment of evil.

• Satan is called *the father of lies* (John 8:44). Satan was the first and greatest liar.

• Satan is called a *murderer* (John 8:44). The Greek word used here literally means "man-killer" (*see* 1 John 3:12,15). Hatred is the motive that leads one to commit murder. Satan hates both God and His children, so he has a genuine motive for murder.

• Satan is called *the god of this age* (2 Corinthians 4:4). This does not mean that Satan is deity. It simply means that this is an evil age, and Satan is its "god" in the sense that he is the head of it.

• Satan is called *the prince of this world* (John 12:31). The key word in this verse is "world." This word refers not to the physical earth but to a vast order or system that Satan has promoted which conforms to his ideals, aims, and methods.

• Satan is called *the tempter* (Matthew 4:3). His constant purpose is to incite people to sin.

From the brief survey of names above, it becomes clear that Satan's avowed purpose is to thwart the plan of God in every area and by every means possible. Toward this end, Satan promotes a world system of which he is the head and which stands in opposition to God and His rule in this universe.

Satan's Vast Experience

It is critical that Christians realize that Satan has vast experience in bringing people down. In fact, his experience is far greater than that of any person. As theologian Charles Ryrie says,

> By his very longevity Satan has acquired a breadth and depth of experience which he matches against the limited knowledge of man. He has observed other believers in every conceivable situation, thus enabling him to predict with accuracy how we will respond to circumstances. Although Satan is not omniscient, his wide experience and observation of man throughout his entire history on earth give him knowledge which is far superior to anything any man could have.[3]

Because of his vast experience, Satan knows what will likely work in his attempt to foul you up. He is a master tempter, with many thousands of years of practice in how to succeed at luring people into sin. *Christian, beware!*

Don't Let the Devil Discourage You

I once read a story that depicted the devil having a garage sale. On the day of the sale, his tools were placed for public inspection, each being marked with its sale price. There was a treacherous lot of implements: hatred, envy, jealousy, deceit, lust, lying, pride, and so on.

Set apart from the rest was a harmless-looking tool. It was quite worn and yet priced very high.

"What is the name of this tool?" asked one of the customers, pointing to it.

"That is discouragement," Satan replied.

"Why have you priced it so high?"

"Because it is more useful to me than the others," Satan said. "I can pry open and get inside a man's heart with that, even when I cannot get near him with the other tools. It is badly worn because I use it on almost everyone, since so few people know it belongs to me."

The devil's price for discouragement was high because it is still his favorite tool. And he is still using it on God's people. Be forewarned: Satan may attempt to use discouragement in your life as a means of neutralizing your walk as a Christian.

"Hell's Angels"—The World of Demons

The demons—also called fallen angels—are highly committed to their dark prince, Satan. Indeed, these spirits, having made an irrevocable choice to follow Satan instead of remaining loyal to God, render him willing service.

Demons are portrayed in Scripture as being evil and wicked. They are designated "unclean spirits" (Matthew 10:1 NASB), "evil spirits" (Luke 7:21), and "spiritual forces of evil" (Ephesians 6:12).

What kinds of wicked deeds do demons do? Among many other things, Scripture portrays them as inflicting physical diseases on people (Matthew 12:22). They afflict people with mental disorders (Mark 5:4-5). They can also cause people to be self-destructive (Luke 9:42).

Of course, we must be careful to note that even though demons can cause physical illnesses, Scripture distinguishes *natural* illnesses from *demon-caused* illnesses (Matthew 4:24; Mark 1:32; Luke 7:21; 9:1; Acts 5:16). So when you get sick, you must not automatically presume you are being afflicted by a demon.

The Work of Fallen Angels

Satan and his host of fallen angels actively seek to harm believers in various ways. For example:

- Satan tempts believers to sin (Ephesians 2:1-3).

- Satan tempts believers to lie (Acts 5:3).

- Satan tempts believers to commit sexually immoral acts (1 Corinthians 7:5).

- Satan accuses and slanders believers (Revelation 12:10).

- Satan sows tares among believers (Matthew 13:38-39).

- Satan incites persecutions against believers (Revelation 2:10).

- Satan seeks to plant doubt in the minds of believers (Genesis 3:1-5).

- Satan seeks to foster spiritual pride in the hearts of Christians (1 Timothy 3:6).

- Demons seek to instigate jealousy and division among believers (James 3:13-16).

- Demons hinder answers to the prayers of believers (Daniel 10:12-20).

What About Demon Possession?

Demon possession may be defined as a demon residing in a person, exerting direct control and influence over that person with certain derangement of mind or body. Demon possession is different than demon affliction. The work of the demon in the latter case is from the outside; in demon possession it is from within.

A person who is demon possessed may manifest unusual, superhuman strength (Mark 5:2-4). He may act in bizarre ways (Luke 8:27). The possessed person often engages in self-destructive behavior (Matthew 17:15). These are just a few of the biblical signs of demon possession.

According to the definition given above, a Christian cannot be possessed by a demon because he is perpetually indwelt by the Holy Spirit (1 Corinthians 6:19). I like what cult expert Walter Martin said: When the devil knocks on the door of the Christian's heart, the Holy Spirit opens it and says, "Get lost!"

It is important to note that there is not a single instance in the Scriptures of a Christian being said to be demon possessed. For sure, there are examples of Christians being *afflicted* by the devil—but not *possessed.*

Christians have been delivered from Satan's domain. As Colossians 1:13 says, God "has rescued us from the dominion of darkness and brought us into the kingdom of the Son he loves." Furthermore, we must remember that "the one who is in you is greater than the one who is in the world" (1 John 4:4). This statement would not make much sense if Christians could be possessed by the devil.

However, we must acknowledge that even though a Christian cannot be possessed, he *can* be oppressed or influenced by demonic powers. But the oppression or influence is always external, not internal. The demons work from outside the Christian to hinder him; they do not work from within him.

The Christian's Defense

We as Christians should be thankful that God has made provisions for our defense against Satan and his fallen angels. What does this defense consist of?

• To begin, twice in the New Testament we are told that the Lord Jesus lives in heaven to make intercession for us (Romans 8:34; Hebrews 7:25). Jesus prays for us on a regular basis. Certainly His intercession for us includes the kind of intercession He made for His disciples in John 17:15, where He asked the Father to keep them safe from the devil.

• God has also provided spiritual armor for our defense (Ephesians 6:11-18). Each piece of armor is important and serves a special purpose. But you and I must choose to put on this armor. God doesn't force us to wear it.

Without wearing this spiritual armor—the belt of truth, the breastplate of righteousness, the shield of faith, and so on—you and I don't stand a chance against the forces of darkness. But with this armor on, victory is ours. Wearing this armor means that our lives will be characterized by righteousness, obedience to the will of God, faith in God, an effective use of the Word of God, and more. These are what spell defeat for the devil in your life.

• Effective use of the Word of God is especially important for spiritual victory. Jesus used Scripture to defeat the devil when He was tempted in the wilderness (Matthew 4). We must learn to do the same. The more we expose ourselves to Scripture, the more the Spirit can use this mighty sword in our lives. If you never read or study your Bible, then you are making yourself vulnerable to defeat and despair. Learn to read your Bible regularly.

• Of course, Scripture tells us that we must be informed and alert to the attacks of Satan (1 Peter 5:8). The apostle Paul reminds us that we are not to be ignorant of his schemes (2 Corinthians 2:11). We find all the information we need about this enemy and his schemes in the Word of God.

• We are also instructed to take a decisive stand against Satan. James 4:7 says, "Resist the devil, and he will flee from you." This is not a one-time resistance. Rather, on a day-to-day basis we must steadfastly resist the devil. And when we do, he will flee from us.

Ephesians 6:13-14 tells us to "stand firm" against the devil. We cannot do this in our own strength, but in the strength of Christ. After all, it was Christ who "disarmed the rulers and authorities...[and] made a public spectacle of them, triumphing over them by the cross" (Colossians 2:15).

• We must not give the devil a foothold in our lives by letting the sun go down while we are still angry toward someone (Ephesians 4:26-27). Such wrath in our heart gives opportunity to the devil to work in our lives.

• We are to rely on the indwelling spirit of God, remembering that "the one who is in you is greater than the one who is in the world" (1 John 4:4).

• We must remember that God has assigned His angels to watch over us (Psalm 91:9-11). As Reformer John Calvin said, God has assigned the angels to "keep vigil for our safety, take upon themselves our defense, direct our ways, and take care that some harm may not befall us."[4] (If you want to understand more about the wonderful ministry of angels, read my book *Angels Among Us*, published by Harvest House Publishers.)

• Finally, we must keep in mind that Satan is "on a leash." He cannot go beyond what God will allow him. (The book of Job makes this abundantly clear.) We can rest secure knowing that God is in control of the universe and Satan cannot simply do as he pleases.

With the help of the guidelines listed above, we can have victory over Satan and his host of demons. And, remember: Successfully defeating the powers of darkness rests upon not what you can do in your own strength but upon what Jesus Christ has already done. You are more than a conqueror through Him who loved us (Romans 8:37). *Keep your eyes on Jesus!*

~~ *A Verse to Hide in Your Heart* ~~

"The LORD is my strength and my shield; my heart trusts in him, and I am helped."

PSALM 28:7

> The church is the body of Christ. Christ
> Himself is the head of this body. The church
> serves and worships Christ.

FOURTEEN

The Church: The Family of God

The church is a company of people who have one Lord and who share together in one gift of salvation in the Lord Jesus Christ (Titus 1:4; Jude 3). The church may be defined as "the ever-enlarging body of born-again believers who comprise the universal body of Christ over whom He reigns as Lord."[1]

Although the members of the church may differ in age, sex, race, wealth, social status, and ability, they are all joined together as one people (Galatians 3:28). All of them share in one Spirit and worship one Lord (Ephesians 4:3-6).

The word *church* is translated from the Greek word *ekklesia*. This Greek word comes from two smaller words. The first is *ek*, which means "out from among." The second is *klesia*, which means "to call." Combining the two words, *ekklesia* means "to call out from among." The church represents people whom God calls out from among the world.

And these people come from all walks of life. All are welcome in Christ's church.

The way you become a member of this universal body is to simply place your faith in Jesus Christ. This body is comprised of *only believers* in Christ. If you're a believer, you're in!

It is appropriate that we include in this book a brief chapter on the church, for the church involves two very important relationships—relationships with other Christians and a corporate relationship with the Lord. One relationship affects the other. If we don't attend church and worship with other Christians, that can have a negative impact on our relationship with the Lord. If we don't have a good relationship with the Lord, that can affect the way we treat other Christians. So it's important that we take both relationships seriously.

The Church Is Owned by Christ

In Matthew 16:18 Jesus affirmed to Peter, "I will build *my* church." This is a foundational truth. The church is not the result of some pastor or priest or body of elders, or some governing hierarchy. It is not owned by some denomination.

It is Christ Himself who builds the church. The church is His and His alone. And Christ doesn't have to clear His decisions regarding the church with any council or church hierarchy. *It's His!*

Christ Is the Head of the Body

Christ not only owns the church, He is also the head of it. He is the head of "the body of Christ." Ephesians 5:23 tells us that Christ is the head of the church (His body) just as the husband is the head of the wife. A husband is to provide for his wife, preserve her, protect her, and cherish her. Christ does the same for the church. He provides, preserves, protects, and cherishes the church as His own.

Ultimately, the fact that Christ is the head of the church is what brings unity to the church. The various parts of the human body move when the brain sends the signal to do so. In fact, the entire body depends on the brain in one way or another. As the brain gives simultaneous signals to different parts of the body, the body functions in unity and is able to go through all kinds of complex motions. Disconnect the brain from the body—such as happens in certain spinal injuries—and body movement is cut off.

In the body of Christ, every member depends upon and should be in submission to Christ, the Head of the body. When each member is "connected" to Christ, the result is a smooth functioning organism. When members "disconnect," or choose not to submit to Christ, dissension arises. In fact, when there is dissension in the church, it is often because one or more "parts" of the body have forgotten that Christ is the head.

A Place of Equipping and Discipleship

I like to think of the church as God's body-building program. Ephesians 4:12 says that a primary role of the church is to equip and disciple church members (that is, build the body) in regard to Bible study, worship, ministry, and much more. If the church fails to equip members in these ways, it is to the detriment of the members.

Chuck Colson, in an interview, stressed how important it is for a church to equip its members:

> If you read Ephesians 4, the job of the pastor is to equip the saints so that when the saints come together in their congregations—for worship, for the study of the Word, for the celebration of the sacraments, for discipline and accountability— they are being discipled by that pastor and equipped for works of service in the world. And by being equipped they can be the light and the

salt that influences the world. This is the whole purpose of the church. The task of the church is to be a place of equipping.

Colson then illustrated the importance of equipping with a story from his past:

> I compare it to my experience in the Marines. I was a lieutenant in the Marines during the Korean War. And that was a very dangerous time. Fifty percent of the Marine lieutenants being commissioned then were coming back in pine boxes. And so, when I went to basic training, let me tell you, I became "equipped" for 18 hours a day—going over that obstacle course, disassembling my rifle, assembling it blindfolded, engaging in night maneuvers, going under barbed wire, learning to survive live artillery shells, and memorizing the *Marine Handbook*. Why? Because I was going into combat, and I was going to have 50 lives in my hands.

"Should we be any less serious about the equipping and discipling of the church?" Colson asks. "No! We're in spiritual combat—cosmic combat for the heart and soul of humankind. We ought to treat it just as seriously as I treated preparing to be a Marine lieutenant in the Korean War."[2]

A Place of Salt and Light

Colson mentioned the importance of becoming equipped to live as "salt" and "light" in our world. The Bible tells us that one of the purposes of the church is to produce Christians who will influence the world for Christ.

Jesus said, "You are the salt of the earth" (Matthew 5:13). Salt is known for its effectiveness as a preservative. We are to have a preserving effect on the world by influencing it for Christ.

Jesus also said, "You are the light of the world. A city on a hill cannot be hidden" (Matthew 5:14). Jesus did not call us to be "secret agent" Christians. We are not to cloak our lights. Someone once said, "No one is a light unto himself, not even the sun." Because the darkness of our world is hovering over humanity as never before, there has never been a time when the light of each individual Christian has been more needed. As evangelist Billy Graham said, "The Christian should stand out like a sparkling diamond."[3] Sparkling Christians are those who take personal evangelism seriously.

A Place of Fellowship

I grew up in a large family of eight kids. That was quite an experience! Because there were so many of us kids, there was always fellowship of some sort among us. No one was ever lonely in the Rhodes house, because there was always someone around.

Likewise, Christian fellowship and sharing should be the family activity of God's people in the local church. And this gathering together with fellowship and sharing gives strength to the people of God. The church, then, is for our benefit. God does not want us to be lone-ranger Christians.

John Wesley, the founder of Methodism, said, "There is nothing more unchristian than a solitary Christian."[4]

C.S. Lewis commented, "The New Testament does not envisage solitary religion; some kind of regular assembly for worship and instruction is everywhere taken for granted in the Epistles. So we must be regular practicing members of the church."[5]

I once read a story about a certain church member who had previously been attending services regularly but suddenly stopped going to church. After some weeks, the minister decided to visit the absent member.

It was a chilly evening, and the minister found the man at home alone, sitting before a blazing fire. Guessing the reason for his pastor's visit, the man welcomed him in, led him to a big chair by the fireplace, and waited.

The minister made himself comfortable and said nothing. In grave silence, he contemplated the play of the flames around the burning logs. After some minutes, he took the fire tongs, carefully picked up a brightly burning ember, and placed it to one side of the hearth. Then he sat back in his chair, still silent.

The host watched all this in quiet fascination. As the lone ember's flame diminished, there was a momentary glow, but then its fire was no more and it was cold and dead.

Not a word had been spoken since the initial greetings. But as the minister rose to leave, the host said, "Thank you so much for your visit—and especially for your fiery sermon. I shall be at church next Sunday."[6]

Billy Graham summarized the point of that story succinctly when he said, "Churchgoers are like coals in a fire. When they cling together, they keep the flame aglow; when they separate, they die out."[7]

A Place of Involvement

The church is a place where every single church member should get involved in serving the Lord Jesus and ministering to the needs of other Christians. The church is not to be a place where the professional clergy does everything. This is not what God intended.

Sitting on the Sidelines

Bud Wilkinson, a famous football coach, was once asked, "What contribution does professional sports make to the physical fitness of Americans?" To no one's surprise, he answered, "Very little. A professional football game," he said, "is a happening where 50,000 spectators, desperately needing exercise, sit in the stands watching 22 men on the field, desperately needing rest."[8] That's also a description of the typical twentieth-century church. Too many Christians stay on the sidelines and watch the clergy do everything.

A generation ago, Dr. F.B. Meyer said this about the need for each person's involvement in the local church:

> It is urgently needful that the Christian people of our charge should come to understand that they are not a company of invalids, to be wheeled about, or fed by hand, nursed, and comforted, the minister being the Head Physician and Nurse; but a garrison in an enemy's country, every soldier of which should have some post or duty, at which he should be prepared to make any sacrifice rather than quitting.[9]

Someone said the local church is like a bank—the more you put into it, the greater the interest. That is really true. If every member of the church got involved in service, their interest level would go up dramatically.

We Need Each Other

One reason it's so important for each person to get involved is that we need each other. Every member of the church has unique gifts and talents given to him or her by God, and each person can render service in ways that no one else can. That's the way God designed it. Each part of the body of Christ is important (1 Corinthians 12:1-20).

The Body of Christ is a lot like the human body in which there are many kinds of cells. There are nerve cells, blood cells, muscle cells, and many others—each having a distinct function in the body. The body operates smoothly not because the cells decide for themselves what they want to do, but because each one does what it was *designed* to do.

Certainly the body would not operate properly if each cell chose to go its own way. A rebellion of the cells in your stomach is called stomach cancer. A revolt of your brain cells is called a brain tumor. Whenever the cells in your body don't operate properly, the body becomes sick.

Many of the problems in the church today result from individual members forgetting that the church is a *body* with each member contributing according to the unique gifts and talents he or she has. We need each other![10]

I read that mountain climbers, for safety reasons, rope themselves together when climbing a mountain. That way, if one climber slips, he won't fall to his death. He'll be held by the others until he can regain his footing.

God designed the church to function in the same way. When one believer slips and falls, the others can hold him up until he regains his footing. Believers in the church are to make every effort to minister to individual members (Hebrews 10:24) and care for the needy in their midst (2 Corinthians 8–9).

A Place of Worship

The church is a place of worship. The word *worship* comes from the old English word *weordhscipe* and literally means "worthship." It denotes the worthiness of an individual to receive special honor in accordance with that worth. The biblical use of the word emphasizes the act of prostration or falling on your knees. A person who kneels before Christ does so because he or she feels that Christ is worthy of such honor and adoration.

Too often genuine worship—the kind that involves vibrant praise and truly worshipful singing—is missing in the church. After attending church with his father one Sunday morning, a little boy, before getting into bed that evening, kneeled at his bedside and prayed, "Dear God, we had a good time at church today, but I wish you had been there."

The combination of praise and song should be a regular part of every church service. Psalm 28:7 says, "The LORD is my strength and my shield; my heart trusts in him, and I am helped. My heart leaps for joy and I will give thanks to him in song." Psalm 69:30 says, "I will praise God's name in song and glorify him with thanksgiving." Psalm 95:2 says, "Let us come before him with thanksgiving and extol him with music and song." Psalm 149:1 says, "Praise the LORD. Sing to the LORD a new song, his praise in the assembly of the saints."

When we get to the New Testament we see this emphasis on praise and song continued. Ephesians 5:19-20 says, "Speak to one another with psalms, hymns and spiritual songs. Sing and make music in your heart to the Lord, always giving thanks to God the Father for everything, in the name of our Lord Jesus Christ." Colossians 3:16 likewise instructs, "Let the word of Christ dwell in you richly as you teach and admonish one another with all wisdom, and as you sing psalms, hymns and spiritual songs with gratitude in your hearts to God."

Of course, because Jesus is the heart of Christianity, much of our worship should be directed at Him. Jesus was worshiped as God many times during His three-year ministry. Thomas worshiped Him (John 20:28). The wise men worshiped Him (Matthew 2:11). A leper worshiped Him (Matthew 8:2). A ruler bowed before Him in worship (Matthew 9:18). A blind man worshiped Him (John 9:38). Mary Magdalene worshiped Him (Matthew 28:9). And the disciples worshiped Him (Matthew 28:17). You and I are called to worship Him!

A Place to Receive Comfort

In my book *Angels Among Us* I recounted a true story that perfectly illustrates the ministry of comfort. It involves something that happened at my church.

Sally could not restrain her tears as she poured out her heart to Pastor Dave. After a series of medical tests, Sally's doctor had called to inform her that the baby she was expecting would be born with Down's syndrome. Pastor

Dave shared Sally's grief at the news. He vowed to help Sally and her husband, Jim, in any way he could.

The following day Pastor Dave decided to send Sally and Jim a postcard with a word of encouragement. On the card, Dave assured them of how much God loved them and their soon-to-be-born Down's syndrome baby.

The postcard ended up being delivered to a wrong address several miles from Sally and Jim's house. Sue—who lived at the house the card was mistakenly delivered to—decided to take the postcard to Sally personally.

When Sally opened the door, Sue said, "This card from your pastor was delivered to my house by mistake. I wanted to come by and deliver the card personally because I, too, have a child with Down's syndrome and I want to help you through this if you'll let me. God has shown me so much blessing that I would like to share with you."

Here's a case in which I believe the God of all comfort sent one of His angels to reroute the mail. God wanted to bring Sally and Jim comfort in their grief.

Sue is the person I want to focus on here, however. Sue was able to minister to Sally and Jim because she had been through the same experience. And she was able to share with this grieving couple the insights she had learned through her experience. Sue was exercising the ministry of comfort.

In 2 Corinthians 1:3-4 the apostle Paul makes reference to "the God of all comfort, who comforts us in all our troubles, so that we can comfort those in any trouble with the comfort we ourselves have received from God" (2 Corinthians 1:3-4). God used Sue as a channel of comfort and blessing through which His own comfort flowed. *This ministry of comfort should characterize every church.*

The church today is full of people who are hurting. And because people are hurting, church members who have already been through specific hurts are admonished to help others who are going through similar hurts. *We need each other!*

Dimensions of Church Growth

My pastor and friend Rick Warren says there are five key dimensions to church growth:

1. Churches grow *warmer* through fellowship.

2. Churches grow *deeper* through discipleship.

3. Churches grow *stronger* through worship.

4. Churches grow *broader* through ministry.

5. Churches grow *larger* through evangelism.[11]

All of these dimensions are important. If the church is missing any one of them, the church suffers.

Fellowship, discipleship, worship, ministry, and evangelism—these elements should be a part of every healthy church. And, ultimately, these dimensions should also come to characterize each individual member of the church.

Are you up for an evaluation? Ask yourself:

1. Is fellowshiping with other Christians a high priority for me?

2. Am I committed to being equipped and discipled as a Christian?

3. Is my life characterized by a worshipful attitude toward Christ?

4. Am I involved in some capacity in the work of ministry?

5. Am I committed to the work of evangelism?

—⚬— *A Verse to Hide in Your Heart* —⚬—

*"Now you are the body of Christ,
and each one of you is a part of it."*

1 CORINTHIANS 12:27

> As Christians, our destiny is to live eternally
> with our blessed Savior, Jesus Christ.

FIFTEEN

Our Future Hope

There is within every human heart a yearning for the eternal. Solomon, in Ecclesiastes 3:11, noted that God "has set eternity in the hearts of men."

The combined effect of a longing for the eternal and a constant awareness of one's mortality causes despair in the hearts of those who have no future hope. For the Christian, however, it is the hope of spending eternity with our eternal God and beloved Lord Jesus Christ that adds meaning to life in the present.

In this final chapter, our goal is to focus together on the future hope of the Christian. I encourage you to not treat this chapter as mere information, but to think of how this information applies to you in your relationship with Jesus.

Man's Natural Fear of Death

Job aptly referred to death as the king of terrors (Job 18:14). The psalmist likewise said, "My heart is in anguish within me; the terrors of death assail me" (Psalm 55:4).

Death is a great enemy of all human beings. It strikes down the good and the wicked, the strong and the weak. Without any respect of persons, death carries its campaign of destruction through whole communities and nations.

There is something in each of us that shrinks back from the very mention of death. After all, God created us to live. Life is natural. But when sin entered the world, the universe was invaded by death. Death is unnatural. Even the apostle Paul—a spiritual giant if there ever was one—considered death the "last enemy" to be conquered (1 Corinthians 15:26).

Except for those Christians who will be instantly transformed into a state of glory at the future rapture, all Christians will eventually go through death's door. As the apostle Paul said, however, death no longer has the sting it once had before we became Christians (1 Corinthians 15:55-57). Because of what Christ accomplished at the cross, and His subsequent resurrection from the dead, we no longer need to fear death's ever-present threat. Because He is risen, *we too shall rise!*

Do you doubt that we can approach death without paralyzing fear? Let me share with you some deathbed statements of Christians in times past. I think you'll agree with me that in their cases, the Lord indeed did take the sting out of death:

- Missionary David Brainerd—"I am going into eternity, and it is sweet for me to think of eternity."

- John Wesley—"The best of all is, God is with us. Farewell! Farewell!"

- Susanna Wesley—"Children, when I am gone, sing a song of praise to God."

- Lady Glenorchy—"If this is dying, it is the pleasantest thing imaginable."

- Pastor John Pawson—"I know I am dying, but my deathbed is a bed of roses. I have no thorns planted upon my dying pillow. Heaven is already begun."[1]

- When Billy Graham's maternal grandmother died, he said the room seemed to fill with a heavenly light. "She sat up in bed and almost laughingly said, 'I see Jesus. He has His arms outstretched toward me. I see Ben [her husband who had died some years earlier] and I see the angels.' She slumped over, absent from the body but present with the Lord."[2]

Truly the Lord has taken the stinger out of death. And because of this, we need never fear death again. *Trust Him!*

What Happens at the Moment of Death?

From a biblical perspective, human beings are made up of both a material part (the physical body) and an immaterial part (the soul or spirit). When a person physically dies, his or her immaterial part departs from the material body.

The New Testament Greek word for death literally means "separation." At the moment of death, man's spirit or soul separates or departs from his body. This is why, when Stephen was put to death by stoning, he prayed, "Lord Jesus, receive my spirit" (Acts 7:59). For the believer, then, death involves his or her spirit departing from the physical body and immediately going into the presence of the Lord in heaven. Death is thus an event that leads to a supremely blissful existence.

For the unbeliever, however, death holds grim prospects. At death, the immaterial part (soul or spirit) departs from the material body and goes not to heaven but to a place of suffering (Luke 16:19-31).

Both believers and unbelievers remain in a disembodied state until the future day of resurrection. And what a glorious day that will be! God will reunite believers' spirits with their resurrected physical bodies. These bodies will be specially suited for living in heaven in God's presence—the perishable will be made imperishable and the mortal will be made immortal (1 Corinthians 15:54). Unbelievers, too, will be resurrected, but they will spend eternity apart from God. (We'll talk more about that later in the chapter.)

The Blessing of Heaven

When Paul had his vision of heaven (2 Corinthians 12:2-4), he heard inexpressible things that he was prohibited from revealing. Apparently heaven is so incredible that God, for His own reasons, forbade Paul to reveal to mortals on earth what lay ahead.

Heaven is an abode of resplendent glory. God Himself dwells there. And though in our mortal bodies we cannot exist in God's presence—though we cannot behold the unapproachable light with earthly eyes (1 Timothy 6:16)—our future resurrection bodies will allow us to do so. And until that day of resurrection, if we should die, our disembodied spirits will go directly into God's presence and enjoy His fellowship.

Christians of all ages have looked forward with great anticipation to the eternal city. Presently we are but pilgrims in a foreign land, making our way to heaven. We can take comfort in this realization!

The City of Glory

In Revelation 21 we find a description of heaven. And what a glorious, splendorous domain it is. Theologian Millard Erickson comments on the splendor of this eternal realm:

Images suggesting immense size or brilliant light depict heaven as a place of unimaginable splendor, greatness, excellence, and beauty....It is likely that while John's vision employs as metaphors those items which we think of as being most valuable and beautiful, the actual splendor of heaven far exceeds anything that we have yet experienced.[3]

Truly, as the apostle Paul said, "No eye has seen, no ear has heard, no mind has conceived what God has prepared for those who love him" (1 Corinthians 2:9). It is beyond human capabilities to conceive of heaven's greatness.

In Revelation 21 we read about the New Jerusalem, the heavenly city in which we will dwell. Verse 23 tells us that "the city does not need the sun or the moon to shine on it, for the glory of God gives it light, and the Lamb is its lamp." This is in keeping with the prophecy in Isaiah 60:19: "The sun will no more be your light by day, nor will the brightness of the moon shine on you, for the LORD will be your everlasting light, and your God will be your glory."

Dr. Lehman Strauss's comments on the Lamb's glory are worthy of meditation:

In that city which Christ has prepared for His own there will be no created light, simply because Christ Himself, who is the uncreated light (John 8:12), will be there....The created lights of God and of men are as darkness when compared with our Blessed Lord. The light He defuses throughout eternity is the unclouded, undimmed glory of His own Holy presence. In consequence of the fullness of that light, there shall be no night.[4]

The Absence of Death

The Old Testament promises that in heaven, death will be swallowed up forever (Isaiah 25:8). Paul affirmed that truth when he wrote about the future resurrection: "When the perishable has been clothed with the imperishable, and the mortal with immortality, then the saying that is written will come true: 'Death has been swallowed up in victory'" (1 Corinthians 15:54). Revelation 21:4 tells us that God "will wipe every tear from their eyes. There will be no more death or mourning or crying or pain, for the old order of things has passed away."

What an awesome blessing this is: There will be no more death—no more fatal accidents, no more incurable diseases, no more funeral services, no more final farewells. Death will be gone and done with, never again to be faced by the people who dwell in heaven. Life in the eternal city will be painless, tearless, and deathless.

Serene Rest

The Christians who are in heaven now are enjoying serene rest in the presence of Christ. They have no tedious labors to attend to. All is tranquil. The apostle John said, "I heard a voice from heaven say, 'Write: Blessed are the dead who die in the Lord from now on.' 'Yes,' says the Spirit, 'they will rest from their labor'" (Revelation 14:13).

For us this "rest" will be a comprehensive rest. There will be rest from all toil of the body, from all laborious work, from all the diseases and frailties of the body, from all outward sorrows, from all inward troubles, from the temptations and afflictions of Satan, and from all doubts and fears. How blessed will be that rest!

Intimate Fellowship with God and Christ

Can there be anything more supreme and more satisfying for the Christian than to enjoy the sheer delight of unbroken fellowship with God and Christ, and have immediate and completely unobstructed access to the divine glory (2 Corinthians 5:6-8; Philippians 1:23)? We shall see our beloved Lord face to face, in all His splendor and glory. We will gaze upon His countenance, and behold His resplendent beauty forever.

Surely there can be no greater joy or exhilarating thrill for the creature than to look upon the face of the divine Creator and fellowship with Him forever. He "who alone is immortal and who lives in unapproachable light" (1 Timothy 6:16) shall reside intimately among His children, and "they will be His people, and God himself will be with them" (Revelation 21:3).

In the afterlife there will no longer be intermittent fellowship with the Lord, blighted by sin and defeat. Instead, we will have continuous fellowship. Spiritual death shall never again cause us to lose fellowship with the Lord, because, for us, the sin problem will no longer be existent. When we enter into glory we will no longer have the sin nature within us. Sin will be banished from our being.

To fellowship with the Lord God is the essence of heavenly life, the fount and source of all blessing: "You will fill me with joy in your presence, with eternal pleasures at your right hand" (Psalm 16:11). We can have confidence that the crowning wonder of our experience in the eternal city will be the perpetual and endless exploration of that unutterable beauty, majesty, love, holiness, power, joy, and grace which is God Himself.[5]

Revelation 21:3 assures us, "Now the dwelling of God is with men, and he will live with them. They will be his people, and God himself will be with them and be their God." God, in His infinite holiness, will dwell among us redeemed human beings because Adam's curse will have been removed, Satan and the fallen angels will have been judged, the wicked will have been punished and separated from God, and the universe will have been made sinless except for the Lake of Fire (Revelation 20:15; 21:8; 22:15).

Reunion with Christian Loved Ones

One of the most glorious aspects of heaven that we can look forward to is our reunion with Christian loved ones.

We are not alone in our longing to join company with those who have preceded us to heaven. The Thessalonian Christians were apparently very concerned about their Christian loved ones who had died. The apostle Paul offered words of comfort in 1 Thessalonians 4:13-17, where we read about the "dead in Christ" and Paul's assurance that there will indeed be a reunion.

And yes, believers will recognize their loved ones in the eternal state.

How do we know this is so? Besides the clear teaching of 1 Thessalonians 4, we are told in 2 Samuel 12:23 that David knew he would be reunited with his deceased son in heaven. He had no doubt about recognizing him.

As well, when Moses and Elijah (who had long passed from earthly life) appeared to Jesus on the Mount of Transfiguration (Matthew 17:1-8), they were recognized by all who were present. Furthermore, in Jesus' story of the rich man and Lazarus (Luke 16:19-31), the rich man, Lazarus, and Abraham were *all* recognized by each other in the intermediate state following death. We can take comfort, then, in knowing that one day we will be reunited with our Christian loved ones!

(For more on what heaven will be like, read my book *The Undiscovered Country: Exploring the Wonder of Heaven and the Afterlife*, published by Harvest House Publishers.)

The Horror of Hell

Everyone will experience life after death. The question is not whether a person will enter eternity, but *where he will spend it*. Those who have trusted in Christ will live with Him forever in heaven. Those who reject Him, however, will spend eternity apart from God in a place of great suffering. That place is hell.

The Scriptures assure us that hell is a real place. But hell was not part of God's original creation, which He called "good" (Genesis 1). Hell was created later to accommodate Satan and his fallen angels because they rebelled against God (Matthew 25:41). People who reject Christ will join Satan and his fallen angels in this infernal place of suffering.

In the Bible, hell is portrayed as a place of horror (Psalm 30:9), weeping (Matthew 13:42), and punishment (Job 24:19). The Scriptures use a variety of words to describe the actual horrors of hell—including fire, fiery furnace, unquenchable fire, the lake of burning sulfur, the Lake of Fire, everlasting contempt, perdition, the place of weeping and gnashing of teeth, eternal punishment, darkness, the wrath to come, exclusion, torments, damnation, condemnation, retribution, woe, and the second death. What horror awaits those who reject Christ in this life!

Unquestionably the greatest pain suffered by people in hell is that they are forever excluded from the presence of God. If ecstatic joy is found in the presence of God (Psalm 16:11), then utter dismay is found in the absence of His presence.

The reality of hell ought to greatly motivate us to share the glorious good news of Jesus Christ with all who will listen. Can you think of someone who needs to hear this good news?

The Future Resurrection

God created man to be not just an immaterial being but a material-immaterial being, with both a spirit and a physical body. Hence, even though having our souls be with Christ in heaven while our body remains on earth is to be preferred over this earthly life, what is even more preferable is to finally receive our resurrection bodies and live in a physical state in God's presence (2 Corinthians 5:4).

From Mortality to Immortality

In our present mortal bodies, we simply cannot exist in the unveiled presence of God. He lives in unapproachable light, and our bodies, as they are now, cannot come before Him.

But all that will one day change. When we receive our glorified resurrection bodies, we will be able to enter God's presence. Just as a caterpillar has to change into a butterfly before he can inherit the air, so also must we change before we can inherit heaven. And once we are changed, we can fellowship with Him face to face.

The apostle Paul tells us, "I declare to you, brothers, that flesh and blood cannot inherit the kingdom of God, nor does the perishable inherit the imperishable" (1 Corinthians 15:50). Paul affirmed that "the trumpet will sound, the dead will be raised imperishable, and we will be changed. For the perishable must clothe itself with the imperishable, and the mortal with immortality. When the perishable has been clothed with the imperishable, and the mortal with immortality, then the saying that is written will come true: 'Death has been swallowed up in victory'" (1 Corinthians 15:52-54). What a glorious day that will be!

A Dramatic Contrast

I think you'll agree with me that the seeds of disease and death are ever upon our present bodies. It is a constant struggle to fight off dangerous infections. We often get sick. And eventually, all of us will die. It is just a question of time. Our new resurrection bodies, however, will be raised imperishable (1 Corinthians 15:42-43). All liability to disease and death will be forever gone. Never again will we have to worry about infections or passing away.

Our present bodies are characterized by weakness. From the moment we are born, the "outer man is decaying" (2 Corinthians 4:16 NASB). Vitality decreases, illness comes, and then old age follows, with its wrinkles and decrepitude. Eventually, in old age, we may become incapacitated, not able to move around and do the simplest of tasks. By contrast, our resurrection bodies will have great power. Never again will we tire, become weak, or become incapacitated. Words are inadequate to describe the incredible differences between our present bodies and our future resurrection bodies.

Developing an Eternal Perspective

Our true significance comes not from the attaining of status and the accumulation of earthly wealth, but from our relationship with Jesus Christ. After all, we will not take our earthly wealth or status with us into the next life. How strange, then, that so many people focus all their energies on building up that which will perish. Modern man, for the most part, has failed to maintain an eternal perspective.

The incredible glory of the afterlife should motivate each of us to live faithfully during our relatively short time on earth. Especially when difficult times come, we must remember that we are but pilgrims on our way to another land—heaven, where Christ Himself dwells.

Gary R. Habermas and J.P. Moreland have come up with a term I like a lot: a "top-down" perspective. That's precisely what we need during our earthly pilgrimage as we sojourn toward heaven:

> The God of the universe invites us to view life and death from his eternal vantage point. And if we do, we will see how readily it can revolutionize our lives: daily anxieties, emotional hurts, tragedies, our responses and responsibilities to others, possessions, wealth, and even physical pain and death. All of this and much more can be informed and influenced by the truths of heaven. The repeated witness of the New Testament is that believers should view all problems, indeed, their entire existence, from what we call the "top-down" perspective: God and his kingdom first, followed by various aspects of our earthly existence.[6]

Our goal, then, should be to maintain a "top-down" perspective. This perspective is a radical love of Jesus Christ that places Him first and foremost in every aspect of our lives. "Set your minds on things above, not on earthly things" (Colossians 3:2). And when we do this, Christ has promised to meet all our earthly needs as part of the package (Matthew 6:33)! What could be better?

～ *A Verse to Hide in Your Heart* ～

"To him who loves us and has freed us from our sins by his blood, and has made us to be a kingdom and priests to serve his God and Father—to him be glory and power for ever and ever! Amen."

REVELATION 1:5-6

Dear friend,

If you have been blessed by this book and would like to know more about "the heart of Christianity," I would be delighted to hear from you.

The ministry I direct offers many materials that can help you grow as a Christian and become closer to the Lord Jesus Christ. I invite you to write:

Ron Rhodes
Reasoning from the Scriptures Ministries
P.O. Box 80087
Rancho Santa Margarita, CA 92688

Reasoning from the Scriptures Ministries is a discipleship ministry that exists to help you grow strong in the Word of God and equip you to become knowledgeable in the application of biblical wisdom.

We publish a free newsletter, and offer a number of other materials (many free) on a variety of relevant issues.

If you would like to be on our mailing list, or if we can be of service to you in any way, please don't hesitate to write.

You can also call us at (714) 888-8848.

The Heart of the Matter

A Christian is one who has trusted in Christ
for salvation and who has a personal
relationship with Him.

~~~

Knowing God should be our chief aim in life.
Jesus has made it possible for us to enter into a living
and vibrant relationship with God.

~~~

God is revealed *in* and *through* the person
of Jesus Christ.

~~~

The God that Jesus came to reveal (God the Father)
is awesome in power and perfect in every way.

~~~

Sin severs our personal relationship with the Lord.

~~~

Whereas sin caused estrangement between
man and God, Jesus at the cross brought
reconciliation and restoration.

~~~

Jesus' words and works demonstrate that He is God.
A personal relationship with Him is the
very heart of Christianity.

~~~

Salvation is a free gift from God and is received by
placing faith in Jesus Christ.

~~~

Our salvation in Christ involves unfathomable
spiritual blessings.

~~~

The goal of the Holy Spirit is to exalt and magnify the person of Jesus Christ in the lives of believers.

~~~

Jesus is our divine Shepherd. He guides and spiritually nourishes all who follow Him.

~~~

Three ingredients that help us grow in our relationship with the Lord are prayer, walking by faith, and reading God's Word.

~~~

The three primary enemies of the Christian are the world, the flesh, and the devil. Christ gives us victory.

~~~

The church is the body of Christ. Christ Himself is the head of this body. The church serves and worships Christ.

~~~

As Christians, our destiny is to live eternally with our blessed Savior, Jesus Christ.

Recommended Reading

If you would like to read more about some of the exciting doctrines of Christianity, you will find some of the following books helpful.

Angels Among Us: Separating Truth from Fiction, by Ron Rhodes (Eugene, OR: Harvest House Publishers, 1995).

A Survey of Bible Doctrine, by Charles C. Ryrie (Chicago, IL: Moody Press, 1980).

Christ Before the Manger: The Life and Times of the Preincarnate Christ, by Ron Rhodes (Grand Rapids, MI: Baker Book House, 1992).

Evangelical Theology, by Robert P. Lightner (Grand Rapids, MI: Baker Book House, 1986).

Jesus Christ Our Lord, by John F. Walvoord (Chicago, IL: Moody Press, 1980).

Knowing God, by J.I. Packer (Downers Grove, IL: InterVarsity Press, 1979).

The Inspiration and Authority of Scripture, by Rene Pache (Chicago, IL: Moody Press, 1978).

The Moody Handbook of Theology, by Paul Enns (Chicago, IL: Moody Press, 1989).

The Pursuit of God, by A.W. Tozer (Wheaton, IL: Tyndale House Publishers, n.d.).

The Undiscovered Country: Exploring the Wonder of Heaven and the Afterlife, by Ron Rhodes (Eugene, OR: Harvest House Publishers, 1996).

Bibliography

Ankerberg, John and John Weldon. *The Facts on Life After Death.* Eugene, OR: Harvest House Publishers, 1992.

Ankerberg, John and John Weldon and Walter C. Kaiser. *The Case for Jesus the Messiah.* Chattanooga, TN: The John Ankerberg Evangelistic Association, 1989.

Basic Christian Doctrines. Edited by Carl F. Henry. Grand Rapids, MI: Baker Book House, 1983.

Berkhof, Louis. *Systematic Theology.* Grand Rapids, MI: Eerdmans Publishing Co., 1982.

Blanchard, John. *Whatever Happened to Hell?* Durham, England: Evangelical Press, 1993.

Buell, Jon A. and O. Quentin Hyder. *Jesus: God, Ghost or Guru?* Grand Rapids, MI: Zondervan Publishing House, 1978.

Buswell, James Oliver. *A Systematic Theology of the Christian Religion.* Grand Rapids, MI: Zondervan Publishing House, 1979.

Calvin, John. *Institutes of the Christian Religion.* Edited by John T. McNeill. Translated by Ford Lewis Battles. Philadelphia, PA: The Westminster Press, 1960.

Chafer, Lewis Sperry and John F. Walvoord. *Major Bible Themes.* Grand Rapids, MI: Zondervan Publishing House, 1975.

Chafer, Lewis Sperry, *Systematic Theology.* Wheaton, IL: Victor Books, 1988.

Connelly, Douglas. *What the Bible Really Says: After Life.* Downers Grove, IL: InterVarsity Press, 1995.

Dickason, Fred. *Angels, Elect and Evil.* Chicago, IL: Moody Press, 1978.

Elwell, Walter A., ed. *Topical Analysis of the Bible.* Grand Rapids, MI: Baker Book House, 1991,

Enns, Paul. *The Moody Handbook of Theology.* Chicago, IL: Moody Press, 1989.

Erickson, Millard J. *Christian Theology*. Unabridged one-volume edition. Grand Rapids, MI: Baker Book House, 1987.

_____. *The Word Became Flesh: A Contemporary Incarnational Christology*. Grand Rapids, MI: Baker Book House, 1991.

France, R.T. *The Living God*. Downers Grove, IL: InterVarsity Press, 1972.

Geisler, Norman. *To Understand the Bible Look for Jesus*. Grand Rapids, MI: Baker Book House, 1979.

Graham, Billy. *Angels: God's Secret Agents*. Garden City, NY: Doubleday & Co., 1975.

_____. *How to Be Born Again*. Dallas, TX: Word Publishing, 1989.

Gromacki, Robert G. *The Virgin Birth: Doctrine of Deity*. Grand Rapids, MI: Baker Book House, 1984.

Habermas, Gary R. and J.P. Moreland. *Immortality: The Other Side of Death*. Nashville, TN: Thomas Nelson Publishers, 1992.

Hodge, Charles. *Systematic Theology*. Abridged Edition. Edited by Edward N. Gross. Grand Rapids, MI: Baker Book House, 1988.

Hoekema, Anthony A. *The Bible and the Future*. Grand Rapids, MI: Eerdmans Publishing Co., 1984.

Hoyt, Herman A. *The End Times*. Chicago, IL: Moody Press, 1969.

Ice, Tommy and Robert Dean. *Overrun by Demons*. Eugene, OR: Harvest House Publishers, 1994.

Keller, Phillip. *A Shepherd Looks at the Good Shepherd and His Sheep*. Grand Rapids, MI: Zondervan Publishing House, 1978.

Ladd, George Eldon. *The Last Things*. Grand Rapids, MI: Eerdmans Publishing Co., 1982.

Lightner, Robert P. *Evangelical Theology*. Grand Rapids, MI: Baker Book House, 1986.

Machen, J. Gresham. *The Virgin Birth of Christ*. New York, NY: Harper, 1930.

McDowell, Josh and Bart Larson. *Jesus: A Biblical Defense of His Deity*. San Bernardino, CA: Here's Life Publishers, Inc., 1983.

Morey, Robert A. *Death and the Afterlife*. Minneapolis, MN: Bethany House Publishers, 1984.

Müller, George. *Autobiography of George Müller: The Life of Trust*. Grand Rapids, MI: Baker Book House, 1984.

Pache, Rene. *The Future Life*. Chicago, IL: Moody Press, 1980.

_____. *The Inspiration and Authority of Scripture*. Chicago, IL: Moody Press, 1978.

Packer, J.I. *Knowing God*. Downers Grove, IL: InterVarsity Press, 1979.

Pentecost, J. Dwight. *The Words and Works of Jesus Christ*. Grand Rapids, MI: Zondervan Publishing House, 1982.

_____. *Things to Come*. Grand Rapids, MI: Zondervan Publishing House, 1974.

Reymond, Robert L. *Jesus Divine Messiah: The New Testament Witness*. Phillipsburg, NJ: Presbyterian and Reformed Publishing Co., 1990.

Rhodes, Ron. *Angels Among Us: Separating Truth from Fiction*. Eugene, OR: Harvest House Publishers, 1995.

_____. *Christ Before the Manger: The Life and Times of the Preincarnate Christ*. Grand Rapids, MI: Baker Book House, 1992.

_____. *The Undiscovered Country: Exploring the Wonder of Heaven and the Afterlife* (Eugene, OR: Harvest House Publishers, 1996).

Ryrie, Charles C. *Basic Theology*. Wheaton, IL: Victor Books, 1986.

_____. *The Holy Spirit*. Chicago, IL: Moody Press, 1965.

_____. *The Ryrie Study Bible*. Chicago, IL: Moody Press, 1986.

Sauer, Eric. *From Eternity to Eternity*. Grand Rapids, MI: Eerdmans Publishing Co., 1979.

_____. *The Dawn of World Redemption*. Grand Rapids, MI: Eerdmans Publishing Co., 1977.

Shephard, J. W. *The Christ of the Gospels*. Grand Rapids, MI: Eerdmans Publishing Co., 1975.

Smith, Wilbur M. *The Biblical Doctrine of Heaven*. Chicago, IL: Moody Press, 1974.

Stedman, Ray C. *Spiritual Warfare*. Waco, TX: Word Books, 1976.

Taylor, Rick. *When Life Is Changed Forever*. Eugene, OR: Harvest House Publishers, 1992.

The New Bible Dictionary. Edited by D. Douglas. Wheaton, IL: Tyndale House Publishers, 1982.

The New Treasury of Scripture Knowledge. Edited by Jerome H. Smith. Nashville, TN: Thomas Nelson Publishers, 1992.

The Zondervan Pictorial Encyclopedia of the Bible. Edited by Merrill C. Tenney. Grand Rapids, MI: Zondervan Publishing House, 1978.

Thiessen, Henry Clarence. *Lectures in Systematic Theology*. Grand Rapids, MI: Eerdmans Publishing Co., 1981.

Tozer, A.W. *The Pursuit of God*. Wheaton, IL: Tyndale House Publishers, n.d.

Vine's Expository Dictionary of Biblical Words. Edited by W. E. Vine, Merrill F. Unger, and William White. Nashville, TN: Thomas Nelson Publishers, 1985.

Vos, Geerhardus. *Biblical Theology: Old and New Testaments*. Grand Rapids, MI: Eerdmans Publishing Co., 1985.

Walvoord, John F. *Jesus Christ Our Lord*. Chicago, IL: Moody Press, 1980.

_____. *The Holy Spirit*. Grand Rapids, MI: Zondervan Publishing House, 1958.

Warfield, Benjamin B. *Biblical and Theological Studies*. Phillipsburg, NJ: Presbyterian and Reformed Publishing Co., 1968.

_____. *The Lord of Glory*. Grand Rapids, MI: Baker Book House, 1974.

Wesley, John. *The Nature of Spiritual Growth*. Minneapolis, MN: Bethany House Publishers, 1977.

Notes

Chapter 1—Just What Is Christianity Anyway?

1. Edythe Draper, *Draper's Book of Quotations for the Christian World* (Wheaton, IL: Tyndale House Publishers, 1992), p. 73.

2. J.I. Packer, *Knowing Christianity* (Wheaton, IL: Harold Shaw Publishers, 1995), p. 60.

3. Packer, p. 138.

4. Draper, p. 66.

5. Draper, p. 66.

6. *More Gathered Gold*, electronic media (Hypercard stack for Macintosh).

7. *More Gathered Gold.*

Chapter 2—Knowing God: The Highest Priority

1. Eric Sauer, *From Eternity to Eternity* (Grand Rapids, MI: Eerdmans, 1979), p. 19.

2. J.I. Packer, *Knowing God* (Downers Grove, IL: InterVarsity Press, 1979), p. 29.

3. Packer, p. 18.

4. Packer, p. 15.

5. In Bruce Shelley, *Theology for Ordinary People* (Downers Grove, IL: InterVarsity Press, 1993), p. 77.

Chapter 3—We Are Not Alone: God Reveals Himself

1. J.I. Packer, *Knowing Christianity* (Wheaton, IL: Harold Shaw Publishers, 1995), p. 10.

2. John Calvin, *Institutes of the Christian Religion*, ed. John T. McNeill, trans. Ford Lewis Battles (Philadelphia, PA: Westminster, 1960), I:53.

3. Packer, p. 16.

4. Packer, p. 15.

5. Based on Charles C. Ryrie, *What You Should Know About Inerrancy* (Chicago, IL: Moody Press, 1981), p. 40.

6. Norman Geisler and William Nix, *A General Introduction to the Bible* (Chicago, IL: Moody Press, 1968), p. 28.

7. E.J. Young, *Thy Word Is Truth* (Grand Rapids, MI: Eerdmans, 1957), p. 113.

8. *Explaining Hermeneutics: A Commentary*, ed. Norman L. Geisler, with Exposition by J.I. Packer (Oakland, CA: International Council on Biblical Inerrancy, 1983), p. 3.

9. John Calvin; cited in Chuck Colson, *Against the Night* (Ann Arbor, MI: Servant Publications, 1989), p. 152.

Chapter 4—Behold Your God!

1. R.T. France, *The Living God* (Downers Grove, IL: InterVarsity Press, 1972), p. 25.

2. A.W. Tozer; quoted in Charles C. Ryrie, *Basic Theology* (Wheaton, IL: Victor Books, 1986), p. 42.

3. *Bible Illustrations*, electronic media (Hypercard stack for Macintosh).

Chapter 5—From Creation to Corruption: Man's Sin

1. Billy Graham, *How to be Born Again* (Dallas, TX: Word Publishing, 1989), p. 118.

Chapter 6—From Corruption to New Creation: God's Solution

1. Robert P. Lightner, *Evangelical Theology: A Survey and Review* (Grand Rapids, MI: Baker Book House, 1986), p. 57.

2. J. Allan Peterson, *Leadership*, 5:2; electronic online version, downloaded from America Online.

3. A.W. Tozer, *The Pursuit of God* (Wheaton, IL: Tyndale House Publishers, n.d.), p. 35.

Chapter 7—The Words and Works of Jesus Christ

1. Jon A. Buell and O. Quentin Hyder, *Jesus: God, Ghost or Guru?* (Grand Rapids, MI: Zondervan Publishing House, 1978), p. 23.

2. Peter Stoner and Robert Newman, *Science Speaks* (Chicago, IL: Moody Press, 1976), pp. 106-7.

Chapter 8—How to Receive the Gift of Salvation

1. *Bible Illustrations*, electronic media, Hypercard stack.

2. Card deck file of illustrations, Dallas Theological Seminary, 3909 Swiss Avenue, Dallas, TX 75204.

3. Card deck file of illustrations, Dallas Theological Seminary.

Chapter 9—The Blessings of Salvation

1. Cited in J.I. Packer, *Knowing Christianity* (Wheaton, IL: Harold Shaw Publishers, 1995), p. 94.

2. *Bible Illustrations*, electronic media, Hypercard stack.

3. Card deck file of illustrations, Dallas Theological Seminary, 3909 Swiss Avenue, Dallas, TX 75204.

Chapter 10—Power from On High: The Holy Spirit

1. R.A. Torrey, *Secret Power* (Ventura, CA: Regal Books, 1987), p. 89.

2. *Bible Illustrations*, electronic media (Hypercard stack for Macintosh).

3. A good place to start is Charles C. Ryrie's book, *The Holy Spirit* (Chicago, IL: Moody Press, 1980).

Chapter 11—Jesus, the Good Shepherd

1. Haddon W. Robinson, *Psalm Twenty-Three* (Chicago, IL: Moody Press, 1979), p. 19.

2. Robinson, pp. 15-16.

3. Robinson, p. 24.

4. Phillip Keller, *A Shepherd Looks at Psalm 23* (Grand Rapids, MI: Zondervan Publishing House, 1976), p. 18.

5. Phillip Keller, *A Shepherd Looks at the Good Shepherd and His Sheep* (Grand Rapids, MI: Zondervan Publishing House, 1978), p. 63.

Chapter 12—Ingredients for a Healthy Spiritual Life

1. Colin Whittaker, *Seven Guides to Effective Prayer* (Minneapolis, MN: Bethany House Publishers, 1987), p. 33.

2. Whittaker, pp. 15-16.

3. Ray Stedman, sermon on Jeremiah 32–33 entitled "Is Anything Too Hard for God?" Peninsula Bible Church.

4. John Wesley, *The Nature of Spiritual Growth* (Minneapolis, MN: Bethany House Publishers, 1977), p. 188.

5. A.W. Tozer, *The Pursuit of God* (Wheaton, IL: Tyndale House Publishers, n.d.), p. 56.

6. John Calvin, *Institutes of the Christian Religion*, ed. John T. McNeill, trans. Ford Lewis Battles (Philadelphia, PA: Westminster, 1960), p. 548.

7. Calvin, p. 549.

8. George Müller, *Autobiography of George Müller: The Life of Trust* (Grand Rapids, MI: Baker Book House, 1984), p. 8.

9. Müller, p. 8.

Chapter 13—Winning Battles

1. *Bible Illustrations*, electronic media, Hypercard stack.

2. Card deck file of illustrations, Dallas Theological Seminary, 3909 Swiss Avenue, Dallas, TX 75204.

3. Charles C. Ryrie, *Balancing the Christian Life* (Chicago, IL: Moody Press, 1978), p. 124.

4. John Calvin, *Institutes of the Christian Religion*, ed. John T. McNeill, trans. Ford Lewis Battles (Philadelphia, PA: The Westminster Press, 1960), p. 166.

Chapter 14—The Church: The Family of God

1. Charles Swindoll, *Growing Deep in the Christian Life* (Portland, OR: Multnomah Press, 1986), p. 339.

2. Chuck Colson, *Christian Research Newsletter*, March 1993, p. 1.

3. Billy Graham; cited in John Blanchard, *More Gathered Gold* (Hertfordshire, England: Evangelical Press, 1986), p. 38.

4. John Wesley; cited in Blanchard, p. 43.

5. *Draper's Book of Quotations for the Christian World*, ed. Edythe Draper (Wheaton, IL: Tyndale House Publishers, 1992), p. 83.

6. *Bible Illustrations*, electronic media, Hypercard stack.

7. Draper, pp. 79-80.

8. Card deck file of illustrations, Dallas Theological Seminary, 3909 Swiss Avenue, Dallas, TX 75204.

9. *Bible Illustrations*, electronic media, Hypercard stack.

10. Card deck file of illustrations, Dallas Theological Seminary.

11. Rick Warren, *The Purpose Driven Church* (Grand Rapids, MI: Zondervan Publishing House, 1995), p. 49.

Chapter 15—Our Future Hope

1. All the deathbed statements are found in Paul Lee Tan, *Encyclopedia of 7,700 Illustrations* (Rockville, MD: Assurance Publishers, 1985), p. 314.

2. Billy Graham, *Angels: God's Secret Agents* (Garden City, NY: Doubleday & Co., 1975), p. 152.

3. Millard Erickson, *Christian Theology* (Grand Rapids, MI: Baker Book House, 1987), p. 1229.

4. Cited in Tim LaHaye, *Revelation: Illustrated and Made Plain* (Grand Rapids, MI: Zondervan Publishing House, 1975), p. 315.

5. Bruce Milne, *Know the Truth* (Downers Grove, IL: InterVarsity Press, 1982), p. 278.

6. Gary R. Habermas and J.P. Moreland, *Immortality: The Other Side of Death* (Nashville, TN: Thomas Nelson Publishers, 1992), p. 185.

Other Good
Harvest House Reading

THE DAILY BIBLE
Compiled by F. LaGard Smith

A quality, softcover edition of *The Narrated Bible* skillfully divides the New International Version into 365 daily readings in chronological order. Devotional narrative guides the reader as God's plan for creation unfolds in uninterrupted sequence.

THE INTERNATIONAL INDUCTIVE STUDY BIBLE

The first of its kind in Bible publishing history. *The International Inductive Study Bible* teaches you how to unearth the treasures of God's Word for yourself. Includes study helps, four-color maps and charts, and a concordance. Available in either the New American Standard or the New International Version text.

THE INTERNATIONAL INDUCTIVE STUDY SERIES
by *Kay Arthur*

The exciting International Study Series takes men and women through a simple, step-by-step approach to discovering Bible truth and putting it into action—using a 13-week format ideal for groups and quarterly classes.

> *Behold, Jesus Is Coming!* (Revelation)
> *The Call to Follow Jesus* (Luke)
> *Choosing Victory, Overcoming Defeat* (Joshua, Judges, Ruth)
> *Free from Bondage God's Way* (Galatians/Ephesians)
> *God's Answers for Relationships* (1 & 2 Corinthians)
> *God's Blueprint for Bible Prophecy* (Daniel)
> *The Holy Spirit Unleashed in You* (Acts)
> *Teach Me Your Ways* (The Pentateuch)

GOD, ARE YOU THERE?
by *Kay Arthur*

In this Bible study for beginners, Kay takes readers by the hand and gently leads them through a study in the Gospel of John as she introduces the inductive method. Includes the New American Standard text of the Gospel of John in its entirety.

Dear Reader,

We would appreciate hearing from you regarding this Harvest House nonfiction book. It will enable us to continue to give you the best in Christian publishing.

1. What most influenced you to purchase *The Heart of Christianity?*
   - ❏ Author
   - ❏ Subject matter
   - ❏ Backcover copy
   - ❏ Recommendations
   - ❏ Cover/Title
   - ❏ Other_____

2. Where did you purchase this book?
   - ❏ Christian bookstore
   - ❏ General bookstore
   - ❏ Department store
   - ❏ Grocery store
   - ❏ Other_____

3. Your overall rating of this book?
   ❏ Excellent   ❏ Very good   ❏ Good   ❏ Fair   ❏ Poor

4. How likely would you be to purchase other books by this author?
   ❏ Very likely   ❏ Not very likely   ❏ Somewhat likely   ❏ Not at all

5. What types of books most interest you? (Check all that apply.)
   - ❏ Women's Books
   - ❏ Marriage Books
   - ❏ Current Issues
   - ❏ Self Help/Psychology
   - ❏ Bible Studies
   - ❏ Fiction
   - ❏ Biographies
   - ❏ Children's Books
   - ❏ Youth Books
   - ❏ Other_____

6. Please check the box next to your age group.
   ❏ Under 18   ❏ 25-34   ❏ 45-54   ❏ 18-24   ❏ 35-44   ❏ 55 and over

Mail to: Editorial Director
Harvest House Publishers
1075 Arrowsmith
Eugene, OR 97402

Name _____

Address _____

State _____ Zip _____

Thank you for helping us to help you in future publications!